My Affair with
Christianity

My Affair with Christianity

RABBI LIONEL BLUE

Hodder & Stoughton
LONDON SYDNEY AUCKLAND

Scripture quotations are taken from the Authorised Version, the text of which is the property of the Crown in perpetuity

The following sources are also gratefully acknowledged:
Father Titus Brandsma, 'O Jesus, as I gaze at you'
John Burns, 'Auld Willie's Prayer'
Sidney Carter, 'One more step along the world I go'
Minnie Louise Haskins, *Desert* (1908), 'God Knows' (quoted by King George VI in his Christmas broadcast on 25 December 1939)

First published in Great Britain 1998
This paperback edition first published in 1999

10 9 8 7 6 5 4 3 2 1

British Library Cataloguing in Publication Data
A record for this book is available from the British Library

ISBN 0 340 66907 1

Typeset by Avon Dataset Ltd, Bidford-on-Avon, Warks

Printed and bound in Great Britain by
Mackays of Chatham PLC, Chatham, Kent

Hodder and Stoughton Ltd
A Division of Hodder Headline PLC
338 Euston Road
London NW1 3BH

To Eric Major, who asked me to write this book
To Leslie Shepard, my teacher
To my good friend in high places

Contents

Acknowledgments

I'm grateful to colleagues and friends who nerved me to finish this book, when my survival instinct told me to ditch it. So thanks also to Rabbi Dr Magonet, Rabbi Hall and Rabbi Solomons, my colleagues; Sister Mary Kelly, Father Gordian Marshall and Father Bill Kirkpatrick, my steadfast friends; Henry and Allan, my Jewish Quakers; Irene Bloomfield, my therapist for twenty years; Theo and Henk, my honest, direct, Dutch friends; Sian who finds things; Peter and Rose, my good neighbours; and Jim, my partner.

No person mentioned on this page can be held responsible for anything in this book.

1

New Beginnings for Old

> In the middle of life's journey,
> I found myself in a dark wood
> and couldn't make out the right way
> forward.
>
> Dante

It has been difficult writing this book. Rabbis are not supposed to have had a Christian experience and if they have had one, they should have the decency to keep quiet about it. But I did have one. I can even say when. It was on a Thursday morning at about half past eleven in November, 1950. I'm going to tell the story of how it happened, why I never became a Christian, and how it led me into the rabbinate!

I decided to set all this down while meditating in the chapel on the floor below my office. I knew I needed a real commitment – like a contract with an advance payment and a delivery date – to make sure I didn't back away. 'Coming out' about physical love, which I had already done, was easier than 'coming out' about spiritual love. It has taken much more hesitation – two steps forwards, one step backwards. I felt so naked describing my innermost inner life.

On the day I decided, I was still a religious bureaucrat –

just – administrating a small canon law court for Reform Jews. I had to deal with the case of the nice, young Jewish boy who fell in love with the nice, young Gentile girl-next-door. Making them feel guilty seemed a dirty trick, and I tried to bridge the gap between reality and tradition as tactfully and unhurtfully as I could. I tried to listen with an understanding heart to the hurt of a divorced couple, who had gone through the pain once before in a civil court, and now had to go through it again in my religious court before they could remarry in synagogue. I had to help my colleagues, who were rightly more into modern counselling than into medieval judging. I had to help them bridge the past and present. But in most things Jewish, even legal ones, joy and food break in, and so did the home-made cakes and coffee of my sympathetic secretary.

Tidying up life's loose debris kept my hold on spiritual truths. You don't need much religion to marry people. Nature does most of the work for you. But you need a lot of God for a clean, generous divorce. It's when formal religion breaks down that spirituality is required. Being a misfit myself, my clients helped me as much as I helped them. I recognised myself in them and in their problems.

But all this structure began to crumble. My secretary and I both developed heart trouble, a sign that it was time to move on. My organisation also wanted a greater legal purity than I thought possible or desirable. All over the world there was a movement for old-time religion and its 'securities'. It even affected progressive move-ments like mine, but I was not prepared to deliver. The gay people I met in bars, the listeners I tried to reach out to through the mike, Hindu and Christian monks with whom I had meditated in silence, and my work in Germany had all blunted my sense of divisions in the human family. Also I was approaching retirement, there was a shortage of jobs and it's better to go before you're pushed.

On the last morning in my job, I locked my desk and told my secretary I needed a breather. She smiled knowingly because she guessed where I was going – to that chapel, hopefully empty, on the floor below, where I could think through the scenario of life that lay ahead of me.

The prayer books in the chapel, (for some of which I was responsible) had copious sections on rites of passage, but it struck me that they dealt mainly with the formal ones. There were no prayers for the unofficial, real ones when you grow up or go to bits; when someone walks out on you for the first time, or you walk out on her or him; when your partner's dead or you're divorced; when you're made redundant; when you receive your first pension payment, or it's your first day in sheltered housing or a Home or a hospice.

I put aside the prayer books and decided to let my thoughts drift. It was an important moment in my life, for ahead was . . . what? Old age (not very nice but what's the alternative?) with its troublesome prostates, dependence, dementia, hair where it shouldn't be and no hair where it should, floppiness where it mattered and even Alzheimer's. Against all these woes I reverted to adolescence and waited for an angel or an adult-in-the-sky to waft out of the ark or out of my imagination, bearing a message. But nothing happened, of course. The power of the magic, myths and fairytales I once enjoyed had weakened. Instead, I gave myself a shake and briskly reviewed my position financially and spiritually. My accountant had briefed me on the first. I wouldn't be rich, but I would be more comfortable than my grandparents or parents had been. Spiritually, I wasn't sure where I was. But that had always been the case. Perhaps I needed to hit the pilgrim road again. Perhaps I had even grown out of religion. Perhaps a smiling Buddha lurked round the corner.

I remembered that rabbis compared this world in spiritual terms to a school and for me the curriculum consisted of two lessons – how to acquire and how to give up. It was the latter now I had to learn. And the hardest parts have to be learnt alone. '*On mourra seul,*' as Pascal said so chillingly.

Or would I die alone? Some lines came into my head from the writer and poet Minnie Louise Haskins, whom few people read now. But during the war everybody had quoted her after King George VI recited them on the wireless.

> And I said to the man who stood at the gate of the year: 'Give me a light that I may tread safely into the unknown.'
> And he replied: 'Go out into the darkness and put your hand into the Hand of God. That shall be to you better than light and safer than a known way.'

My purposeless musing began to irritate me. Being Jewish, the best therapy for me was work. That was what I was put in this world for. But I now had to find my true work inside myself. I could no longer use office routine as a substitute. The first thing to do was to get started on the unfinished bits of homework I'd avoided. Many years ago I wrote an autobiography: *A Backdoor to Heaven*. I said at the time that I had taken off six veils, and later I unveiled a little more, but I had never been ready to divest myself of the seventh, to add to it. Well, unless that one came off now to complete the other six in a 'full monty', it never would. I decided that I would ring my agent, who would ring my publisher and I'd go wherever the resulting striptease led me. Underneath that final veil was sex, but that's not news these days. More disturbing would be the revelation of what and whom I'd met in my imagination long ago and the account of the rebirth of love within me.

When I got back to my office I made that phone call, and my secretary remarked how much more cheerful I looked. Religion feels right when it gives me courage to face a muddle I'd prefer to suppress. I hope it helps all those who have touched the radioactive core of another faith like me. Good on yer, God! God on yer, Blue!

2

A Morning-after-the-Night-before Experience

I started to think back to that Christian experience when I was at a party which was just breaking up. Now, parties are fertile places for memory and spiritual insight. Like the departure lounge at Gatwick Airport, for example, or the concourse at Euston Station, they seem so secular that no religious expectation clogs them. This leaves space for the unexpected to get in and for unscripted spiritual insights to happen.

Religions can be born at parties. A Buddhist once told me this story in a hospital waiting-room. The Prince Gautama, he told me, once woke up at a party in the first light of dawn. With his head propped on his elbow, he considered the contorted bodies, pasted together by sex and drink, the snores, the grunts, the spilt wine. Then, softly treading between the sleepers so as not to disturb them, he left the banqueting hall and the life that went with it, exchanging his royal robes for the cloak of a homeless hermit. Retiring to the shade of a Bo tree, he meditated on the cause and nature of happiness and unhappiness and was 'enlightened'. It is the supreme example of the 'morning-after-the-night-before' experience which is familiar to every Soho carouser, enterprising student at Oxford, or determined drunk on a pub-crawl. Buddhism, one of the largest and most profound ways of spirituality on earth, is built upon it.

Important turning-points in my own life took place at parties. At a teenage party I watched the boyhood friend I loved being introduced to the nice girl I knew even then he would marry – though they didn't – and for the first time felt adult pain. Standing outside myself as it were, I watched myself shrivel into myself; a small, contorted ball of jealousy.

At another party, when I was still at Oxford, I met the guru and analyst who redeemed me from institution-alisation or suicide. I was forlornly singing along to a wind-up gramophone. 'No man can use you when you're down and out,' wailed the gramophone and boy! did I know it! He responded to my hidden wail, surged out of the shadows and promptly fixed an appointment for me.

And at a card party, being no gambler myself, I watched with curiosity the passions stirred up by poker and liar dice. I saw that the spiritual world stands in the same relation to the 'real' world as the 'real' world does to the passions packed into a pair of dice.

And it was when a party was on its last legs that the subject of this book began to form in my mind. Why I had been invited to that party I cannot remember, nor why I had accepted, being at least two generations older than anybody else there. But I was content and interested since watching another generation is more foreign and exotic than anything you bump into abroad. Also, en-sconced near the smoked salmon, I could munch and meditate at the same time.

A few guests had already left, mostly in pairs. But some sat or lay beside each other, mildly petting or confiding political opinions as a prelude to more committed

petting – the men trying to refill the girls' glasses, and
the girls deftly defeating the age-old strategy. I noted that
some of the girls were liberated and practised role-
reversal, filling the glasses of their too slow boyfriends.

A single man like me, but younger, came and sat beside
me. I could tell he was gay, since all minorities suss out
each other. He asked me, politely, if my affur was present?

'My what?' I stared at him puzzled, befuddled by two
gins and his northern accent. Affur, affur, *affaire*? I got it!

'Oh, I don't think my partner would like to be called
that,' I answered primly. My partner was old-time I said,
like Greer Garson in *Mrs Miniver*, or Celia Johnson in
Brief Encounter. And I explained gently to the young
man that my partner, my affur, had made it brutally clear
at the start of our relationship that we were either
exclusive or nothing – no *affaires*, affurs or whatever,
and I was really too old to prowl through gay bars again
as the oldest swinger in town.

But the single man did not want to pick me up, as I
wondered quite unnecessarily. He just wanted to talk
about himself, like any healthy youngster, and I was
content to listen, marvelling at the honesty and directness
of his generation. I compared it favourably to my own
which was too furtive and screwed up to accept self-
knowledge. The clergy had been the most screwed up
because of all the role-playing they have to carry out to
keep their jobs, risking their integrity.

However, the young man was talking and I was being
discourteous. He had never tried for a gay marriage like
me, he said. It felt unnatural, like living in a straitjacket
or corset. Perhaps when he was old (and past it) . . . He
discontinued this line of thought lest I take offence, which
I didn't – after sixty-five, realism wins over romance
hands down.

He had had more than a few affairs in his young life, and though a few had ended – really ended – most had changed, transformed and settled down into solid friendships. The partner he had loved longest and most deeply had now married and he had become godfather to the children. There had been no dissimulation. His former lover's wife understood the strength of feeling that underlay their friendship and did not resent it. Some of his former loves still lived on their own like him or were shacked up with other lovers, whom he had befriended too. In fact, nearly all had remained good friends even when sex no longer lubricated their relationships. I complimented him on his talent for friendship, which I truly envied. I told him how I had only recently learnt how to remain on good terms with an ex, without feeling obliged to whip up an unnecessary drama of rejection, or an inquisition of fault-finding.

There is no service to celebrate friendship in church or synagogue service books (and I know because I have written some). But in big towns the families of blood were dispersing, while new families of friends were forming and replacing them. It was friends whom you rang up when you were ill, who celebrated your successes with you when you were up and who commiserated with you when you were down. I enthusiastically told the young man that he had no need to feel guilty for the life he described, which amused him, as such a thought had never entered his mind.

I thanked him for telling me about his way of life, which puzzled him, but though he could not know it, he had lifted some spiritual unease from me. For though I had tried to be exclusive sexually, in spiritual matters it had been otherwise.

The introduction of such a dimension puzzled him and

I tried in turn to explain my spiritual life, which intrigued him. I had been married to Judaism all my life, I told him. In some ways it resembled an arranged marriage because I had been born into it. I had never chosen it. It had chosen me, and anti-Semitism had burnt it into me. So it was part of me whether I liked it or not, like my family, or my circumcision – the 'covenant cut into my flesh' – which I could do nothing about. Though what had started as a fact of life had gradually turned into quiet, deep love.

But this had not stopped me falling in love and, like him, having affairs with other loves, some of which had stayed with me all my life, though they were spiritual or ideological in nature. Both of us knew you can never get rid of those you have loved. Your loves lodge in you if you give them room. Lodged in me were my Marxist affair, with its processions; and my anarchist affair in underground coffee bars; followed by my Quaker affair with its clean silence, and my Anglo-Catholic affair with its incense; followed in turn by my psychoanalytic affair with me horizontal, and my Vedantic one with me meditating on images in clean, white undies. All these I had once loved and still do. But it was my Christian affair which had pushed me into the rabbinate. It was my only love affair for many years, even though my lover was only see-through. But it kept me sane when I nearly exploded with frustration. Only after many years of regular, physical love did that see-through lover of my imagination transform into my friend who lived within me and merged into me.

But I was like this young chap, my new acquaintance; one manifestation of love was never enough for me. The claustrophobia of creeds and codes always felt like a straitjacket. So I had always slipped through the theological nets so artfully laid for me by ecclesiastical

11

establishments, because there was too much truth outside all of them, and I was a wanderer and wonderer by
temperament. So I had never joined 'the Party', nor fallen
into any font (circumcision I couldn't help because I was
too young to have had any say in the matter) even though
at times I longed for such security. Establishments,
whether religious or political, never like this sort of
behaviour. For them it is disordered, unstable, idiosyncratic, deviant and lots of other high-class swear-
words. I take their point because for thirty years or more
I have been part of an establishment myself and know
how difficult it is to keep the show on the road.

Conversion, of course, can be coped with, provided
that as the convert commits himself to new Brand X he
also forswears all the truths of old Brand Y, his former
love. Converts are not allowed to take much luggage with
them across ideological or spiritual frontiers.

My new acquaintance looked at me thoughtfully while
I rambled on, debating with myself and fighting
fantasy battles like a suburban Don Quixote, and said
he would get me another gin. And during his absence I
decided to set down the story of my inner life; even the
bit, *especially* the bit, which would get me into most
trouble: my wandering into the no-man's-land which
separates Judaism from Christianity. It was an awful
mess and I must settle down and work it through. I
sighed. Was that a job for a Yiddisher boy? Poor Blue!
Parbleu!

I exited from the party, carefully treading a straight
line and stepping over the sleepers like the Buddha. My
considerate hosts, and the nice young man whose sexual
life had so much in common with my spiritual one,
decanted me into a taxi. Had I been bored? they asked
solicitously.

A Morning-after-the-Night-before Experience

'Oh, no, not that,' I said. 'A lot is revealed at parties when you allow yourself to let go inside as well as outside. Good night! Good night!'

3

Ju-Jew in Many Flavours

> And as [Paul] journeyed, he came near Damascus:
> and suddenly there shined round about him a light
> from heaven: And he fell to the earth, and heard a
> voice saying unto him, Saul, Saul, why persecutest
> thou me? And he said, Who art thou, Lord? And the
> Lord said, I am Jesus whom thou persecutest . . .
>
> Acts of the Apostles 9:3–5

Unlike Paul's, my Christian experience did not just fall
from heaven. It had roots in my restless childhood, its
own prehistory. For Christianity was not my first faith.
Before I met Christianity I had had many loves, like the
man I met at the party, and all of them had remained
with me and still do. I inherited my first from my Russian
grandmother but thought I'd lost it at the age of five. It is
still the one I love most.

This was the way of it. Two years after I was born, my
mother was taken to hospital with an obscure blood
illness. While my father looked for work, my mother's
mother mothered me. She handed on to me her medieval
mix of superstition, self-sacrifice, piety, mysticism,
prayer, faith and food. Her religion was holy and haunted
both by angels and demons. Under her instruction I gave
to the poor, honouring them as the closest I would ever

get to bumping into God. Even now I have difficulty in walking down a West-End street without an orgy of compulsive giving. I also learnt to spit three times whenever I received a compliment, as she did lest the surrounding spooks got jealous. And I learnt mantras and prayers to placate the powers that be, and sensed the visitors from outer space clustering round our Sabbath candles. She looked on benignly while I avoided the cracks between paving-stones or touched things, as do many insecure children and even adults. She was the most loving, anxious woman I have known, and when she died I withdrew into myself, being an only, lonely child.

My parents did not come home till late. My mother worked late while my father searched London looking for work. In the meantime, I was supposed to attend religion classes where we learnt by rote in the medieval manner. Questions were not encouraged, and doubts were squashed. I preferred my own company in the darkening, empty streets of London's East End. There I developed two other-worldly relationships. One was with the moon, which moved with me wherever I went; and another was with an angel, whose light I sensed haloing the gas lamps and lapping round street corners. Those early 'friends' showed me wonders. The moon silvered the puddles and rimmed our tenements with magic. So I encountered beauty. The angel drew me into another world, holier and kinder than anything I knew here, and holiness and kindness have remained real for me ever since. My 'friends' lived in my imagination but they were not nothings. The adults I knew then lived on illusions they gained from films; my communist uncle lived on the illusion of a workers' paradise in Russia; and religious people I know still mostly live on myths about events which never happened, or which never happened in the way they believe they happened, except in their imagination.

All this collapsed at the age of five after my grandmother died and I started going to school. Though Jewish children are surrounded by love, little is kept from them. Early on, I was acquainted with unemployment, the dole, cancer, Mosley and Hitler. Being a pragmatic child but uncertain how to deal with the outside world, I prayed for the speedy demise of the two last who were terrorising our little Jewish community. Their followers threw old people through windows, and daubed insults on our houses. According to Grandma, if you prayed hard enough for something holy, it would happen. Well, it didn't! I saw their photos in a newspaper a few weeks later, flourishing like the bay tree. As I had suspected since going to school, Grandma's medieval recipes didn't work for faith, only for food. So, holding the hand of my uncle, I marched with the Reds instead, because they were scientific and knew what the world was about. Prayer didn't change anything in the material world around me. It was magic which didn't work, prescientific juju. This I still believe.

What was left? A memory of holiness and generosity, a compulsive neurosis which has taken years to get rid of, an inner world of the imagination tenanted by the moon and angels.

My new Marxist ideology was also a religion. Like any devotee or believer I could lose myself in it. As I didn't like my self, this seemed the best thing I could do with it. Marxism was intensely moral, even prudish, and demanded the mind and heart. Two dreamy, idealistic relations went back to the USSR to help build the new Utopia. They were never heard of again. We never knew which gulag they died in or whether they were killed off by Stalin or Hitler. Cousins also fell in the Spanish Civil War. Good was at war with evil and, in the coming apocalypse, the former would overcome the latter, the Republic of Goodness replacing the kingdom of God on earth. This was scientific! It was also a good preparation for the New Testament apocalypse I encountered later. Both were developments of intertestamental Judaism.

Marxism was also a good preparation for established Christianity because it was obsessed with purity of doctrine, authorised scriptures, heresies, orthodoxies, schisms, and lines of authority. Later on, when I got involved in arguments about the heresy and orthodoxy of the new churches, I felt completely at home. It was the same music, transposed to another key.

Although the comrades were not very good at liberty, this was a relief because I wouldn't have known what to do with it. Equality was something we all acknowledged but didn't practise – like Stalin being a comrade like us or the Pope being just 'the servant of the servants of God'. Some comrade, some servant! It was fraternity that I really longed for, a lovely, sticky, toffeeish feeling you felt in processions, which were an accepted though unmentioned form of sublimation. I first thought communion did the same thing for Christians, but then I realised it wasn't meant to stick you to other people and make you a groupie, but to absorb God spiritually within you.

Marxism was a light that failed for me because its psychology was too crude. Marxism preceded Freud, but unlike more sophisticated religions which had learnt over the centuries to absorb and adapt, it never developed any mechanism for the purification of motive. As an East German professor said to me, the revolution was hijacked by personal motives, such as ambition, paranoia, hunger for power and so on. It always is! (There were some attempts at repentance ceremonies in the Chinese cultural revolution but these were primitive compared to the religious rituals with the same aim.)

So early in 1950, marching in a procession which was bawling the names of Communist leaders, I suddenly asked myself what I was doing in it. This wasn't rational. This was idol worship and all the Jew in me revolted. It was cruder juju than poor old Grandma's. I left the procession, dived into an Indo-Pak restaurant and – fortified by two portions of curry – ceased to be a Stalinist/Marxist and never marched for anyone again. But an unofficial Marxist I remained. Marxism left its inheritance lodged in me. I still adhere to its universalism and the brotherhood of human beings. Miracles are still not part of my world whatever their label, Jewish or Christian. I assume that even the most rarified mysticism has an economic or social dimension. And I am still moved by the vision, 'from each according to his ability, to each according to his need'. That remains my social ideal. Another faith had hit the dust, but not quite. Like the lovers of the young, gay man I had met at that party, a part of it survived in me. The love affair ended and the starry eyes clouded, but some of it had become part of my mind and changed the way I thought.

It was difficult knowing where to go after the comprehensiveness and mass exaltation of Marxism. At first, I went to the other extreme, to its disestablished, heretical mirror-image: idealistic anarchism. In cellars in central London and obscure coffee bars, I met a new set of comrades and was reminded of my grandmother because of their sheer goodness. They were honest, too, in a way established cults and ideologies never were. They were the only ones who were open about sex, even homosex, and I listened astonished. Neither religion nor Marxism could cope with it or even dare mention it, and their ideologists and priests ran a mile when I did. They disappeared over the horizon so fast that I rightly suspected their attachment to truth. The anarchists were the first and only group I met who weren't furtive. But then they had no power, poor dears, so could not be corrupted by what they never had.

This is why I sadly bade them goodbye. They believed in the natural goodness of people and I wasn't so optimistic. Also, part of me liked establishments and power and slogans and dressing-up. I just wasn't good enough for them. Religion seemed more realistic because it deals with sinners.

My idealistic Zionism also got wrecked on universalism and homosex. To take the latter, for example; for people who were building the great new society, their social attitudes remained suburban – albeit Suburbia by the Med. Also, I felt uneasy sublimating sex into nationalism. That was the most dangerous of all. Nationalism, my youth leaders said, would lead to internationalism. I wasn't so sure. They gave me a wonderful Jewish education, but my promised land was really Bohemia. I couldn't get to Greenwich Village, which was its capital, but I finally made it to Amsterdam. When I entered my first gay bar, I knew my body at least had come home!

That gay bar and Marxism taught me a lot, though the latter would not like to have acknowledged the former's company. In both I met Gentiles, non-Jews, *goyim*, and made a great discovery – that some of them also possessed a Yiddish heart and Yiddish compassion, just as I knew Jews who possessed neither. Rosa Luxemburg was Jewish by origin, but Liebknecht and my other adolescent saints, Prince Kropotkin and Rudolph Rocker, weren't. The Holocaust was not just Jews versus the rest, but good against evil, light against darkness, progress against reaction. My Marxists and anarchists had made me a citizen of the world and I could never go back to a ghetto again.

As I surveyed the wreckage of past ideologies, I did what my parents wanted me to do – go to Oxford and get a middle-class education with social standing. They didn't know it, but I went there to find out the recipe for revolution. And a revolution did happen that neither they nor I expected, within me, not outside me, beyond both our expectations.

4

What the Bells Said

Oyf'n priputchik brent a feierle
Un in schtub is heys.
Un der rebbe lerent kleine kinderlech
dem alef-bayss.
In the oven burns a little fire
And the room grows warm.
And the rabbi teaches little children
To learn the holy Hebrew alphabet.

A song of the Jewish East End of London
written in Yiddish by Max Warschawsky

Christianity first lodged in my consciousness as I stag-
gered out of Oxford Station. The station hadn't been
rebuilt after the bombing, and I clutched an ex-army
rucksack and a broken suitcase, stuffed with my bits. I
remember a battered squash racket I was too astigmatic
to use, which nevertheless looked classy.

As I stumbled and bent down, reassembling my bits, a
bell pealed above me, and then another, and then another.
It was a kind of welcome. I looked up to see their source
and became engrossed in the strange skyline of Oxford,
punctuated by spires like exclamation marks, all pointing
up, heavenwards.

The animist bit of me wondered what all those bells wanted to tell me, and I shook myself physically to be free once and for all of the spooky inheritance left in me by Grandma. I was rather shocked that this centre of learning, where I would learn to predict the future by analysing the past, should be sunk in the superstition and mythology I had left the East End to escape. 'More class superstructure!' I thought – I should have known it.

That's what the Marxist part of me said. But another part of me said, 'Hey, hey! Look at all those churches around you. This is like the Yiddish holy city of your childhood, where every block had its little Hebrew school and prayer room, and our Jewish life was cocooned in their piety.' Was life here cocooned in Christian piety?

This was a puzzle. I had gone to Oxford to prospect the future, but this was a return to my childhood, before I had seen those pictures of Hitler and Mosley thriving in the daily paper.

And once the thought lodged in my mind, I couldn't hear anything but bells. Christianity seeped through to me from all directions – from Latin graces, plaques on walls, theology bookshops, from the church beside my bedroom, against which students piled up gravestones to climb in. I already knew something about Christianity, which I had picked up from school prayers; from chance meetings with dedicated worker priests while hitch-hiking; from a server at St Mark's in Venice who gave me the glad eye during Mass; and from discussions with fanatical, Evangelical students in youth hostels, eager to win a soul for Christ – mine too, because quality didn't count, only quantity. And in my rucksack I used to pack Bunyan's *Pilgrim's Progress* because I had read it at junior school and it had lodged in my mind. Even when I was a Marxist I still wondered if my physical journeys were enfolded in a metaphysical one, though I never dared tell this to the comrades.

Most of my new comrades – the chaps on my staircase who came from minor public schools – considered themselves 'Christian'. They came to tea with me to urge on me the rival claims of Ow-queue and Oy-queue, which I later deciphered as OUCU and OECU, the former meaning 'smells and bells', and the latter, Evangelicals.

I pondered their rivalry with relief. All talk at that time in spiritual circles was centred on the validity of orders in the Church of South India, just as the Marxists were all het up about Lysenko. I was catholic enough to comprise both. The former was far more fun as I didn't give a damn either way. I just marvelled how much this new Christianity recalled my Marxism. There was the same appeal to sacred scripture, to tradition, to validity; the diabolisation of opponents as deviationists, heretics, traitors and schismatics. My former fulminations against Trotsky could be turned to ecclesiastical use, which pleased me because I dislike ideological waste. In between adolescent masturbation, I mused on the validity of the Church of Sweden. Their orders certainly derived from a Catholic bishop, but he was bonkers! Christian polemics and politics were familiar stuff. It was like playing bridge. There were only a limited number of moves and insults and you could turn them any way you wished. The left could agonise over serious things like Academician Lysenko. I was going to have some fun!

It was while sitting in Balliol library, translating the Latin of the Venerable Bede's *Ecclesiastical History of the English People*, that Christianity seeped through to me in a very different way. It began to dawn on me that we Jews, my Jews, might not be the only ones to have a holy history.

Their England, my England, might have one too.

This disconcerted me because the set books of the Oxford history syllabus are meant for analysis, not for faith. But something in those pages turned me on – the ardour of Celtic saints, the simple response of Anglian kings. Bombs were going off in Belfast, and yet here something Christian could cross a racial chasm. I wondered at the generosity of Bede who could overcome his Roman prejudices to report it all in a golden glow. I hadn't met such generosity since I moved among anarchists and mourned the death of Rudolph Rocker, the non-Jewish German who gave his life organising the Jewish sweat-shop workers of New York.

As I translated passages in tutorials, I was lifted out of the world of exams and marks and interviews into an affair of the heart. I didn't want to précis them, I wanted to pray them, which I did, much to my room-mate's disgust. They still touch me, those stories of the conversion of the northern semi-barbarian kingdom with its warrior kings, into holymen, martyrs and saints.

Though these passages were fresh, I cannot say they were new – just unexpected. Giving was, after all, familiar territory, for Jews give more to charity per head than any other community in this country. My grandmother gave the little she had to her unemployed neighbours and marching miners. I remembered Marxists, anarchists and Zionists who had given their lives.

What was new was a special kind of giving – giving up. What to make of Aidan and Cuthbert retreating to rocks in the North Sea, not giving to anybody, just giving up? Why did they give up every human comfort for the grim, grey cold of a Northumbrian winter? What good did it do them? What good did it do anybody? What were they doing it for? For God? But what did he get out of it? I needed an answer to understand medieval history. But this was not the whole truth. I needed an answer to understand myself, because something in me wanted to do the same. I wanted to give away and give up too. Though what I couldn't imagine!

The need was so urgent that I even travelled to Lindisfarne off the Northumbrian coast to gaze on the few stones that were their earthly remnants, in order to intuit their purpose. Why did renunciation, austerity, asceticism and giving up attract me? I read Thomas Merton and recognised the same longing in him. My world was beginning to turn inside out. I was being sucked into Christianity.

Then something brought all these bits together. A prayer burst out of me at a Quaker meeting. It was the simplest and sincerest prayer one can ever utter: 'Help!'

5

Help!

I had stumbled into the Quaker meeting by chance, as I came back from what was intended to be a mild, morning, petting session in a girl's room in her college. It was a fiasco for the poor girl and me. The sky was grey outside and I felt grey inside. I only entered the meeting house because it was starting to rain. I later learnt that the meeting was for local people. Their straightforward testimony, unlike the more convoluted convictions of students, so moved me by its unexpectedness and direct-ness that I ejaculated a loud cry at the meeting (it was the first I ever attended). It was like a scream, or like the stopper exploding from a ginger beer bottle. I had attended that meeting only because of a mistake. But something was set off in me, because I got to my feet and testified.

I do not remember exactly what I said but it must have been powerful stuff because the other Friends were as shaken as me and I got invited to tea by the chairman – Miss Joachim. An honour! Sublimation had rocketed me into high spiritual circles.

I was even more shaken because I actually thanked God for my accursed problems. 'I know now,' I said, 'that they are my spiritual capital, disguised blessings, which could help other poor sods like myself.' Since I never mentioned my sexual hang-ups, just my spirituality, I never quite believed in its reality because it couldn't bear the weight of honesty. But then no religion could at that time. And quite a lot can't bear it still.

The honest part of me, which I've never been able to suppress, knew there was a bit of flaunting in my testimony, some spiritual swanking, more spiritual truth than factual honesty and a dollop of megalomania. There was also something else in it which had yet to reveal its hand. I later realised it was the topsy-turvy paradoxes of the Gospel parables which began to turn things inside out in me and which kick-started my Christian experience.

I joined the many preachers who are hypnotised by their own sermons, which doesn't mean there isn't something important in them. My spiritual blow-out felt like bliss, the answer to a maiden's prayer; and I was still a maiden more or less, albeit an unwilling one.

Something did happen after that inner prayer and outer testimony. Not exactly an 'answer', because I am cautious about 'answers'. I am a post-Holocaust Jew, painfully aware of the wagonloads of human misery on their way to the camps and gas chambers. How many prayers must have been said or sobbed in them, which were never answered in any way that made sense to those who prayed them. A God who 'answers' the prayers of a neurotic like me, or the occasional sufferer at a shrine, but who didn't release those Jews from their misery is a God too frivolous and erratic to worship.

But something can happen (not an 'answer') when you are desperate enough to be sincere, when life has so dented your self-satisfaction that there is room for something else to enter, when you're so humbled you begin to know what you don't know, and you no longer know in advance what will result from your cry. Without this stripping, this turning inside out, you do not pray – you attend services.

The prophet Jeremiah talks about a game of holy hide-and-seek. I found it in classical fundamentalist fashion when the Bible fell open on that page before me. A wonder? No! But a dial, a pointer, because my inner thoughts seized on it? Yes! 'When you call and come and pray to Me, I will hear you. When you seek Me, you will find Me, if you search for Me with all your heart. I shall let you find Me, says the Lord' (Jeremiah 29:12–14). The key words are 'with all your heart', and even then it is you who change, not the world outside you.

At the time of writing this book, my greatest source of spiritual refreshment comes from HIV and AIDS retreats which I help organise. It is not I alone who say this but the others who attend and the sisters who run the retreat house. Things happen at those retreats because those taking part are not playing about with the frivolities of religion. Like me at Oxford, they too are crying, *'Help!'*

6

My Life Turns Inside Out

I knew by the time I went to the Quaker meeting that the bells which had greeted and confused me outside Oxford Station were the tip of an iceberg. They did have a message for me, and the curiosity that had gripped me as I parsed Bede's Latin in Balliol was a pebble that began to release an inner avalanche.

I had heard Christians talking about their conversion experiences. Was I having one now? I wondered, because at that Quaker meeting the world began to turn inside out, spinning like the sun at Fatima.

I was unprepared for what would happen next. Perhaps a miracle would clinch the situation. I fluttered my eyelids at altars but only got an eyelash under my eyelid. In any case, if God had produced a miracle for me when he hadn't shown his salvation during the Holocaust I would have been deeply disapproving. But I did start to see the world differently before and after my testimony. It was like the difference between black and white TV and colour TV, or more like the difference between any kind of TV and reality.

The paradoxes of the Gospels began to work in my mind like yeast: a failed messiah; losing your life in order to gain it; the last being the first and the first last; heaven being a place where you served, not where you were honoured. The Oxford syllabus turned inside out too and became a puzzle because 'successes make you clever but only your failures make you wise'. Should I still strive for a first?

True, my experience hadn't saved me from the things Christians are supposed to be saved from – hell, sin and death. But being Jewish and Marxist, those things didn't bother me anyway. Not even death, only pain, for life had got so muddled that I didn't have that much to lose. When I left that Quaker meeting, I knew I had been saved from my own bitterness. Halleluiah! And I am not being cynical.

As that bitterness drained out of me, a most unexpected inside out took place. I felt myself becoming younger and less like a wizened old man. I started to enjoy myself, Jewish style. I never expected a Christian experience to help me enjoy this world and Jewish jokes. I thought it would do the opposite because it seemed such a tormented, screwed up religion. But I began to enjoy people and the world we lived in seemed very funny, often hilarious, though the humour could be decidedly black. This wasn't just a 'high' after a depression because it has remained that way ever since, and no 'high' lasts nearly fifty years.

In the days that followed, whatever caught my attention seemed to turn inside out as soon as I examined it. The pushing queues in shops became souls like me lining up for paradise, and they seemed beautiful. It was just like the moon gilding the puddles with light as in my childhood, or the aura of angels metamorphosing an East End street into a divine highway. Many times I just wanted to go on my knees and gasp thanks for the glory of it all. It was a curious mixture of real insight and a neurotic high and I hadn't the slightest idea how to separate them.

But what about the obstacle to my childhood faith which had turned me away from religion fifteen years before? That turned inside out too, like everything else. I realised fuzzily that, as Simone Weil said more succinctly when I came to read her later, in this inside out world, prayers are boomerangs because we are the only hands God has in this world. His only power is the love he inspires in us. There is nothing else on offer. As the rabbis said, the reward of goodness is more goodness and the reward of evil is more evil. But I only realised they had said that after I returned to Judaism.

One proof of the change in me was that the centre of my ego was gradually shifting. I now got more joy out of giving than receiving. I liked giving up my seat on crowded trains – it was like a lover giving a present he could scarcely afford. I liked giving so much that I didn't know where to stop, and no Christian could tell me. I tried, for example, to cook all the meals during the vacation but my room-mate said, 'I know I can't cook as well as you, Lionel, but do you have to take away all my self-respect?' He added that the next time I tried to exercise my soul on him, all the food would go into the dustbin. I cringed.

Later on, life and death turned inside out too, after another Christian experience. This helped me live this life more efficiently. I ceased to expect things from it which it couldn't give.

Everything was turning inside out so fast that I got frightened. I was no longer in control. I would either end up as a father in a Carthusian monastery or with the mother of all breakdowns. Being basically Jewish in outlook I chose the latter but part of me is still attracted to the 'death in life' of the former. It does make Christian sense.

I also have to admit that my academic work went to pieces during this time, and my Christian experience didn't have the slightest effect on my sexual desires or my sexual outlet. It was just like Marxism – sublimation didn't work.

Was there any proof for all this inside out stuff? This was the question of common-room conversation. I tried to bluster it out, quoting philosophers and theologians none of us had ever read, such as Karl Barth. We'd only just heard about him. But really they were irrelevant, only I was too insecure to admit it. The only proof I would ever have was me, and the slight shift in my ego. That is faith!

7

'Comin' for to Carry Me Home'

I looked over Jordan and what did I see?
Comin' for to carry me home.
A band of angels comin' after me,
Comin' for to carry me home!

Spiritual

You'll get pie
When you die
In the sky
(chorus) It's a lie!

Left-wing student song

From the age of five I sang the chorus 'It's a lie!' fervently
on Marxist processions, bellowing it out as a kind of
accusation. The second effect of my Christian experience
was that I got heaven back. I got no pie with it, just a
home, which I needed far more.

Like most Jewish families in this century, my own
relatives have also been 'wandering Jews', changing their
language and culture, searching for countries which
would let them in and allow them to live a decent life. So
home has always been uncertain. As a child, I never took
it for granted. The insecurity was part of daily life. We
were poor and so we rented rooms. Both the bailiff and

the rent-collector were grey eminences in our lives. At school, children discussed their devious movements. We could sense the rising tension among our parents as they made their probing rounds and enquiries.

My mother could generate enormous willpower when she was determined. So after she and my father got jobs again, she set her heart on and obtained a whole house which had bugs but no hot water or indoor loo. It was her dream house, with an American cocktail cabinet without cocktails, and was much admired locally. But Hitler was even more determined than my mother and one morning, as we came out of the shelters to make sure our house was standing, it wasn't. There was just a black hole. So my mother commandeered a barrow and wheeled our bits to the lock-up for bombed-out people like us.

I have never believed in the permanence of solid houses since. Nor, in fact, do many Jews. Some still leave a corner of their living-room unplastered to show they also know, like Augustine, that here is no abiding city. To this belief was added the confusion of the evacuation years, when I transferred from 'home' to 'home', each one with a different set of foster 'parents' or 'uncles' and 'aunties'. All had their own domestic rituals. In some, you had to pull the chain at night; in some, only for solids not liquids; in others, never, and God help you if you chanced to release a noisy Niagara . . .

I've always tried to make a 'home' like my mother, suppressing experience and common sense for the sake of make-believe. It's my Jewish instinct. Instinctively, I tried to make a 'home' for all my committed relationships in the Jewish manner, hoping to make them permanent that way. But when the relationship was dying the home became a prison, and when it actually died only a house was left. I still make a private pilgrimage to visit those places occasionally. I stand outside them trying to work out what happened, what went wrong in me. One was a late-Victorian three up, three down; another a yacht ('as our boat sinks slowly in the west . . .'); then a flat by the Med.; and then a terrace house up north. Looking into the not-too-distant future, I shall have to think about a different sort of home, then a hospice, and then my eternal home. That's life!

Human need produces not only religion but also escape and fantasy, and all three are related and entwined. They take a lot of therapy to disentangle. There were my childish compensation fantasies – in which home was a palace, without bugs and with endless hot water. There were the B movies running around in my mind – in which I continued the happy endings of films like *Tophat* and home was the Ritz of my imagination. Then there followed the puberty fantasies – in which I shared a thatched home on a desert island with a troop of older lads.

There was something else, though I didn't know how to place it. An old boyfriend of my mother's unexpectedly gave me an anthology of English poetry and, because my parents wanted me to get out of the ghetto, they encouraged me to find poems and recite them. To their consternation, I fastened on a poem by Francis Thompson. I couldn't understand the long words, nor could my parents, but I intuited their meaning.

> O world invisible, we view thee,
> O world intangible, we touch thee,
> O world unknowable, we know thee,
> Inapprehensible, we clutch thee!

All of us were intrigued by the idea in a later verse of

Jacob's ladder being set up 'betwixt Heaven and Charing Cross', because we used to celebrate in Lyons Corner House nearby. But what really got my parents was the last verse, which referred to Christ walking on the water. I didn't mind leaving it out because I didn't believe it, so therefore it didn't interest me. The first verse did, though, because it drew me home.

Later on, I read George Herbert's poem, 'Love', and understood intuitively again the experience of a spiritual dinner for two.

But into my Oxford loneliness came the parables of the kingdom of heaven that I found in the Gospels. I came upon them in Blackwell's bookshop. I was attracted by their title and brooded over them because they didn't seem to be fairy stories like so much else in the Scriptures. I went along with some but not with others, puzzled about their subject matter until a piece of the jigsaw snapped into place. When they talked about heaven, they were really talking about home. The reason I didn't know the way to go home was because I was looking for it in the wrong way and in the wrong dimension. Home wasn't what or where I thought it was.

Home was permanence, stability and love; not walls, roofs and interior decoration. The former are things which the external surfaces of reality cannot provide. I had to see beyond and behind the surfaces of this world, backing the hunch in the Gospels that the 'see-through' was more real than the surfaces. It was yet another instance of 'inside out' which I was just beginning to recognise everywhere, so I was no longer surprised.

In the Gospels, the kingdom of heaven was not beyond the stars or where you grow 'roses that cannot wither' (I had never believed in them anyway), but tucked away in the common household articles and experiences of domestic life. It was the light under a bushel, the lost penny. The doors to the kingdom weren't spectacular but everyday and all around me, which is why I had never noticed them. But how to enter through them?

Quietly, at a Quaker meeting house in Oxford and again in a silent priory, I found myself within those doors just like that, without thinking or trying. I went into that meeting house a rootless refugee and came out more secure than houses, because I had come home, though for the life of me I didn't know where it was or what it was. It is the nearest I have ever come to a religious experience. This lingered on in me for quite a time because I lived in my heavenly home. Though I then found myself out of it as unobtrusively as I went into it, it has never left me. I still retain my toehold in heaven. It wasn't far beyond the stars or anywhere. It was bliss. Another text clicked: 'The kingdom of heaven is within you.' So now I knew where it was; it was in me. I didn't just think the parables, I experienced them.

I knew I had come home as soon as I opened my eyes at the meeting. The people there, the tables, the chairs seemed perfect. Everything was still and newly created just as it was meant to be. I saw with the same eyes as Vermeer when he saw his 'View of Delft'. I could see with innocence. The anger in me had somehow been unblocked. I even became giggly. I had been so serious before and I now realised what a joke it all was. This was not a normal Christian response and the other worshippers were taken aback by my unexpected amusement, but Hindu friends understood. It's strange that such a heavy religion as Christianity could produce such a lighthearted result. It did it to St Francis, too.

This experience was not a fantasy. Because of it I saw

the real me, the real world and my place in it. I saw that this world was not a permanent place and never could be – it had a lot in common with the departure lounges of airports. You made yourself as comfortable as you could and struck up friendships – some of which could go deep – but it was no use seeking permanence in it or security – it wasn't that kind of a place. Once I was reconciled to its nature, life became less muddled. I didn't manipulate people around me into absurdities ('How much do you love me?' 'Promise me you'll never leave me!' 'We'll always be as we are now', 'I'll become this or that and never change'). I enjoyed people more and used them less. Some friends of mine came to this naturally. Only from my toehold in heaven could I glimpse reality, both inner and outer.

I thought a lot about heaven and still do. (Later on, I found that lots of rabbis wrote parables about the kingdom of heaven and Jesus was only one of them.) Most of my books mention heaven in their titles and I can't help humming popular songs about it. It can't be an after-life because when we die, time and space die with us. Despite all the Christian 'evidence', I agree with the rabbi who said, 'Since nobody has returned from the dead, nobody knows anything about it.' But I do know there is a 'Beyond Life' (not an after-life) in some reality I cannot understand, which is the source of our souls and all goodness. And that Beyond Life can be experienced now if you are open to it. Music turns the experience on for some. For others, charity or generosity does. For me and others, it occasionally comes as a free gift. At an Oxford cocktail party, standing with a glass in one hand and a canapé in the other, and talking non-stop, a part of me would step out of me and would look down on me and everybody with overflowing compassion. Walking along a street I would suddenly step into it. It wasn't a place or a time but another dimension of reality, of being; another gear.

Later, I found I could make heaven happen if I did something for the sake of heaven, or used the logic of heaven which is not based on the calculations of the ego. It could reveal itself in an impulse of uncommon sense. Heaven could also die in you if you didn't cherish it. Then you would say it was irrational, foolish, unworldly, good material for a therapist. But you knew in your heart you were losing something of great value. A sense of loss remained which wouldn't go away. A rabbi gave me a card which I put on my office desk. It said, 'If you believe in me, I exist.' Heaven is like that.

This was my new home. I didn't know it; I recognised it again because it was with me in my earliest childhood when my grandmother was alive. It pulls me towards it like gravity.

Later on, I encountered a rabbinic story which confirmed what I had read in the Gospels. A man asks to see heaven. His prayer is granted. To his astonishment he sees only some sages studying.

'But that's exactly what they did on earth!' he cries out in disappointment.

'Don't you understand?' comes the reply. 'The sages are not in heaven, heaven is in the sages!'

Nobody talked about heaven in the Jewish circles I encountered at Oxford. After the Holocaust, our problem was survival in this world. The continued existence of Jewish life in Europe hung by a thread. But for me personally a one-way ticket to Tel Aviv was not my journey home. I tried it and it didn't work. In fact I felt more uprooted there than in England, and the Palestinians worried me. I needed to go behind and beyond life in this world to another world, another mode of living, to make sense of life in this one. It was the Christianity I encountered at Oxford which came to carry me home.

8

Jesus Who?

O Jesus, as I gaze at you,
I feel again my love for you,
and that your own heart's love for me,
makes me your very special friend.

I know the suffering that love brings
and that such suffering does me good
because it makes me more like you,
and brings me to your kingdom.

> Written by Father Titus Brandsma in 1942,
> in Scheveningen Prison, after he had
> been arrested by the Nazis.

The twelve march on with martial tread,
a limping dog brings up the rear,
a blood red flag flies overhead,
and marching with them in the van,
is Christ Jesus, son of man!

> Alexander Blok

All of this turning inside out and making a home in heaven
might have remained just another ideology that enlightened me when I needed some kindly light in the
gloom that encircled me. I had already known quite a

few which moved me deeply. But this was different, because it caught me up in a cosmic love affair. Which is why this *affaire* marked me more deeply than my previous ideological affairs. It brought together so many parts of me – the sexual part, the mystical part, and the dreams of childhood which I thought had gone for ever.

The childhood fantasies – the angel and moon – came alive in me again and reformed themselves into the same Jesus who appeared to the Christians around me, which was both surprising and not surprising. This is a cautious way of putting it. My feelings at the time were not so clear-headed. Whether he was the creation of my needs, or a deep part of me, or from the farthest reaches of the cosmos, I couldn't care or decide. I did decide to fall in love with whatever, whoever, because there wasn't anybody else.

He answered so many of my needs; tailor-made you might say, and many did say. But this didn't make any difference, because my needs were overwhelming.

In the first place, he was the answer to a maiden's prayer. I was more or less a maiden, more rather than less unfortunately, and not through choice. I was also very lonely because I was bad at relationships. Because I was so demanding, prospective partners got scared. Jesus was all sorts of things. He was the brother I'd prayed for; the only one who understood me; the lover I longed for but had no hope of getting, who loved me more than I loved him; the rabbi who didn't preach at me; the kind wise teacher I always wanted; the constant companion who would save me from loneliness. I was also the ventriloquist and he was my dummy – almost, but not quite.

And he did save me in part! Not from conventional Christian fears but from being poisoned by the dark within me. Some say anger and hate are only love turned back on itself which cannot find an object. He was my love object, and for the first time in years my love flowed freely. He didn't do it alone. Later, I had other love objects – my dogs and a partner – and years later still, therapy purified my inner anger by helping me understand it.

My Jesus-figure was very like me – too like me to be comfortable. He was the nice part of me. He was a young man like me but slimmer with chestnut curls; quite a cutie. He also had too many fathers, like me, and trouble with his strong-minded mother, like me. If I had said to my mother what he said, 'Woman, what have I to do with thee?' my God, there would have been a set-to. She would have hit me! He was unmarried like me, and I thought he might be homo like me (a bishop thought so too). The whole set-up seemed so Jewish.

A Jewish joke – and there are Jewish jokes about everything in heaven or on earth – put the likeness to my set-up succinctly. A Jew says to a Christian, 'Yes, I think Jesus was very Jewish.'

'I'm pleased you say that,' says the astonished Christian. 'But as a matter of interest, why do you think so?'

'It's simple,' said the Jewish man. 'He went into his father's business, he only left home when he was thirty, he was convinced his mother was a virgin, and she was convinced he was God.' That was true for the Blue family and the Holy Family.

Socially, Jesus came from my class too, the artisan Jewish lower-middle class. I know Christians like to think he was the poorest of the poor, but that is their romanticism and inverted snobbery. Beneath his family at Nazareth, who had local standing, there yawned the abyss of the dispossessed peasants, and beneath them the unrecorded slaves. He wasn't quite Golders Green but he was certainly Hackney or Stoke Newington. For that matter, I was born in a Salvation Army hospital, and we couldn't get into an inn or boarding house at Margate. Jesus and I had a lot in common. Whether he came from outside me or inside me; whether he was real, a myth or a dream; I didn't know or care. It wasn't relevant at that time. Being a pragmatic person who had always coped with a surfeit of beliefs, I decided that it would have to work itself out in my subconscious, theology or visions. I had more immediate concerns than its provenance. When people asked if he wasn't really me, I replied that he was 98.7 per cent me and let them puzzle over that.

This sounds outrageous, but it isn't really so. Lots of priests and other celibates come to their vocation as an answer to a maiden's prayer. And their Jesuses are mostly them too. In religion, it doesn't matter where you start but where you finish. Everybody goes into it for the wrong reasons. The reasons purify themselves out in time if you're honest about them.

Like the poet Gray, I soliloquised in a churchyard, while chewing gum on a bench, figuring out how many Jesuses I knew. There were so many it was mind-blowing, and all of them were sincere. The Christians I knew made a good case for him as a Quaker, a Baptist, as Anglo- or Roman Catholic. I remembered a poem from my Marxist days when the poet Blok made a case for him as a Communist fellow-traveller, marching with the ragged, heroic Red Army. But obviously Franco considered him a fellow-travelling Fascist too. Even Hitler had his own Christian theologians and his Nazi Church. The dismal fact was that you could make a case for all of them and make him anything. He could be establishment C. of E. or anti-establishment hippy.

Such Jews as did consider him also used him as a kind

of mirror without realising it. Some stressed that he was a pious, orthodox Jew who kept far more commandments than present-day modern rabbis like me, which was true. Others said he was a reform or liberal Jew ahead of his time, and they had a lot of right (or left) on their side too. Some said he was a Jewish nationalist but that this had been edited out by the early Christians after the fall of Jerusalem to curry favour with the Romans. Some said he was just a Jewish socialist but this had been edited out to please Gentile and Jewish fat cats by Paul. Both ideas were possibly true. Who could say? Most Jews said it was all Paul's fault. And I thought this too until I read the mystical passages in Paul, which are overwhelming and rather dangerous. I listened to the contending parties with increasing unease, but in the churchyard I decided that clear proof was impossible. It was all a good preparation for the tangles of the Talmud, which came later.

One priest tried to answer these points by saying Jesus was so humble that he allowed us to make whatever we liked out of him. This had possibilities, but as a one-time materialist, I found it too subjective to trust. Far more important to me was what I made out of him, and more intriguing was what he made out of me.

So what did he give me? As I've said, he was my love object who turned my bitterness inside out and gave me a new lease of life. By linking my love life to religion, he turned religion into a love affair, not just an ideology; an ethic, a code, a pattern of behaviour, a recipe for group survival. By finding someone to love, all the pent-up feelings in me were released and the crooked in me became straighter. He made me nicer on the whole, which is the test.

Did I believe in him? That is a Christian question which I didn't know how to answer. Probably not in the

Christian sense. I only knew that 'by their fruits ye shall know them', so I'll try and set out what those fruits were for me and what they weren't.

He was certainly very pliable. As long as I wanted a lover he was my lover – in so far as you can be one if you're see-through. We could hold hands, as it were; cuddle a bit, as it were; kiss a bit, as it were; smooch a bit, as it were (Grrr . . . all those 'as it were's). But there it had to stop until I became see-through myself.

He helped me a lot later on, when I had a solid lover who was convalescent for many years. We lived in a limbo-land which was at first supportable and then far more than supportable because Jesus was with us too. It seemed a dead time but the three of us were together – four counting my dog – so there were moments of glory and quiet happiness beyond anything I had ever expected. Again, things turned inside out. My convalescent partner got up late. I sat silent in empty chapels, and my figure was in the silence and supported me. He had changed now into a friend, one of the best.

He had also changed in appearance. The blond and chestnut curls became black like my own. He also ceased to look pious and constipated as in Christian iconography, but was sharper and more mischievous. The pseudo-Aryan kitsch peeled away and he became plumper like me.

Then, instead of always seeing him outside me and separate from me, I began to see him in other people. He was Janusz Korczak who went with the Jewish orphans of the Warsaw ghetto into the camps and gas chambers. He was the image seen by Father Titus Brandsma in the Scheveningen Prison in 1942. He was Anne Frank. Later, I began to see him in the unworthy as well as the worthy, and later still I began to see him in me. Then I no longer saw him, only the kindness and the courage and as a pointer to my Beyond Life. Like the Cheshire cat, only the smile was left. It was like the Emmaus story in the Gospel. You don't notice whom you meet in life. Only later you add two and two together and make a glorious five. Then things begin to turn inside out and heaven opens up.

This is a long way round to state a simple observation. People incarnate what they worship. If you love someone, you begin to become like them – you can't help it. That is why couples begin to look like each other and pet owners start to resemble their pets.

When I studied Judaism systematically, it surprised me to discover how much a religion which was anti-image actually used images itself as I did in my imagination. This was true not so much in fastidious modern times but in older, more pious times. In the Hebrew Scriptures, of course, God is known through physical and psychological anthropomorphisms which are used freely and easily. The biblical writers don't bother with get-outs like 'as it were' or 'in common parlance'. God has hands, a mouth and a backside like us. He is also angry, jealous, joyous and murderous like us too. In the traditional liturgy, rampant anthropomorphisms feature in medieval hymns. Some modern editions leave them out; some shrink them to small print, but they can't be got rid of because of their holy provenance and antiquity.

His head all shining with the dew of light,
His locks all dripping with the drops of night . . .
His head is like pure gold. His forehead's flame
is graven glory of His holy name . . .
His hair as on the head of youth is twined,
in wealth of raven curls it flows behind . . .

> Ruddy in apparel, bright He glows
> when He from treading Edom's wine press goes . . .
> (from Service of the Synagogue – New Year)

They go beyond anything I ever thought up! Whatever the philosophical or theological rights and wrongs, you can only know the unknown by some analogy to what you know. Many people can't begin to understand the intensity of the love of God unless they have loved a fellow creature with all their heart too. With me, it was the other way round. It was only after I loved the divine that I began to understand how to love a fellow human being.

Also, since the 'kingdom of heaven is within you', it is impossible to separate God from yourself. Was all this a case of my normal self beginning to embrace my better self? Me loving me? I don't know the answers even now, and probably never will.

9

Another Holy History

> And did those feet in ancient time
> Walk upon England's mountains green?
> And was the holy Lamb of God
> On England's pleasant pastures seen?
>
> **William Blake**

'Mummy, mummy, I don't want to go to America!'
'Be quiet, darling, and keep on swimming!'

That extraordinary term at Oxford ended. The winter weather was bright and clear and I turned myself into a pilgrim. To absorb that experience I had to accompany my inner journey with an outer one. So I hitch-hiked across England, taking occasional country buses, trying to puzzle out that inside out experience in pilgrim places and meeting dead people who had done the same. It started off as a forage through history. It quickly became a journey into my soul.

An unexpected effect was that it naturalised me into my own country. Until then, I had always assumed I was English because of my accent, which was steadily growing more Oxford. I felt superior to my grandparents who would always be foreigners, despite their intense gratitude to this country. But now I knew there was a layer of England into which I had never penetrated: its religious past. This is a problem for members of most immigrant communities, who can't handle it and so push it aside. They do this because that religious past can only be a Christian past, which is a problem because it could compete with their own religious present. My Christian experience forced me to relate to England's holy history. Having two holy histories leaves an identity problem. I'm pleased I worked through it, because it enlarged me not just for history and Oxford exams but it also affected my soul, for the deeper test of life itself. Every minority is tempted to skip the exploration of Christianity in England, but to look at this layer of the past does not mean conversion – only complexity and ultimate enrichment.

My grandparents came over to England around the turn of the century. They were one droplet in the great waves of poor and persecuted who were trying to reach America, the *goldene medina*, the Yiddish for 'golden country', God's own country. Some made it, some were turned back tragically at Ellis Island, some half made it and never got further than Britain. Some didn't even know they never made it, like my grandmother, who rarely ventured outside her kitchen and was never sure whether this was America.

When war was declared in 1939, it became important to know the nationality of my grandfather. Otherwise he might be sent to the Isle of Man as a 'friendly enemy alien' or some other sort of alien, though he had lived here since boyhood. Finally, he went to the Soviet embassy, who grudgingly issued him with a red Soviet passport stamped *'forbidden to return to the Soviet Union'*. It was a pretty useless document, but it satisfied the bureaucrats and at least let him survive in Stepney during the blitz. He personally considered himself 'Breeteesch' and, though he was an idealist anarchist, he felt a personal loyalty to the King-never Edward VIII whom he distrusted, but to King George VI.

My parents inherited his personal patriotism but were more integrated into British society. They spoke Yiddish only when they didn't want me to understand (so I learnt to understand a lot of it). They were proud to be real-born British and displayed the Union Jack and my coronation mug. This wasn't show. Great Britain had rescued them from the horrors of Russia, tsarist and Stalinist. As for me, I went one step further and thought of myself as English, though the Nazi persecution had raised doubts in my mind. What would happen here if the Nazis invaded and won? Would I be handed over to them as just another foreign Jew, as some would be in the Channel Islands?

I thought I had solved my own identity problem until I went to Oxford. There I stumbled across a whole dimension of it that I had never encountered – England's Christian spirituality and religion. This was not one particular denomination or sect within it but all of it. It's not necessary or desirable to become Christian in order to become English but I personally had to assimilate and integrate that dimension into my Jewish belonging, in order to feel rooted in the country of my big blue passport.

From my Christian experience, I realised that we Jews were not alone in having a holy history. England had one too. As Blake knew, Jerusalem didn't only exist in the Middle East. The Holy City also dwelt in the hearts and minds of English mystics and English workers. Christianity was the key that opened a door to the presence of

God in the history I was studying. That presence had already started to change my thinking and my life, and one of its side effects was an inner naturalisation.

This did not come about for social or economic reasons. I wasn't fleeing from my Jewish belonging. I had no illusions about the anti-Semitism I encountered in Belloc, Chesterton, Buchan and T. S. Eliot, whose work I read at school. There was an upper-class kind and a lower-middle-class kind. I had experienced both. One day I might also have to flee to a 'national home' if one still existed. This deeper relationship came about from love – the love of God, who had appeared to so many people in the very places I now lodged in and visited.

There was my fascination with the 'giving up' of Celtic and Saxon saints. But there was more, much more. I discovered all this as I criss-crossed the country with my rucksack. Heaven came very close when I dropped into unadorned compline or evensong in an English country church. It felt very intimate. Sometimes I was the only person in the congregation, which made it even more intimate. Sometimes the silence of Quaker farmers' meetings made me want to cry at the holy simplicity I had stumbled into. In 1950, I saw in my imagination the figure of a medieval Jesus arching across the sky, giving meaning to my fragmented life and drawing the new housing estates into himself.

I used Bunyan's *Pilgrim's Progress* as my travel guide. With it I hitch-hiked through Vanity Fair, struggled to escape from Doubting Castle, chatted with Mr Valiant-for-Truth, and hesitated on the banks of the River Ouse at Bedford, Bunyan's river of death. I nearly got bitten by a swan! I crossed that river, again in my imagination, not with Christian but with Miss Much-Afraid because like her I was subject to anxiety attacks. I also saw how you could lay down the worries of this world if you had faith in the next. I didn't know if I had it but I now knew that another dimension, another gear, existed and what it could mean in a human life.

This strange, erratic pilgrimage through the English past introduced me to dead people who were even odder and more disorganised than me. In my imagination I conversed with them, and they became the fast friends I needed. I had to journey to meet them. At home it wasn't possible. I had to make the effort to meet them on their territory. You don't get something for nothing in the spiritual world either.

My company of saints, official and unofficial, had a practical effect on my life. In pubs I remembered the poems of William Blake, who contrasted the warmth of pubs and alehouses – always open – against the cheerless places of worship, where you couldn't worship because they were locked up. Jesus had a soft spot for publicans, and I did too after I watched one of them that Christmas let an old lady nurse an empty glass so that she could stay in the smoky warmth till closing time.

In Lichfield, I read how Dr Johnson stood in the pouring rain at the place where his father tried to sell books that no one would buy. My father had tried to sell ice cream in winter during the slump and I had been embarrassed by his failure. When I got back to London I stood outside a tea stall where he used to warm himself and shelter against the rain. I just said, 'Sorry, Dad!' Unfortunately, he died before I understood his sacrifices for me. But that 'Sorry!' helped me if not him. Did it help him? I didn't have enough faith to be sure.

Hitch-hiking from Manchester, I took tea in Knutsford, because Mrs Gaskell based her *Cranford* on Knutsford. I can nearly quote by heart its first page even now: 'In the first place Cranford is in the possession of the Amazons . . .' It is the kindest novel in the English language. From it I learnt to see God at work in the lives of a few elderly, old-fashioned ladies, whose class was soon to be swept away in the Industrial Revolution. They were more real than the doubtful virgins of early Christian history, going on and on about their virginity and its miraculous insurance. I never believed in them, anyway. As my secretary used to say, 'And the band played "Believe it if you like", Lionel!'

My best and most surprising friend was Margery Kempe, a fifteenth-century housewife and entrepreneur who was even more neurotic than me and just as sexy. I admired her honesty when she admitted having made an assignation for adultery after, not before, her vision of Jesus. That's the way it is. I went to see the place where the adulterer stood her up in King's Lynn church. Having been stood up myself I knew the feeling. Like her, I also preferred Jesus to God the Father (like my mother I never could abide beards), especially if he sat at the bottom of my bed. But her love was validated when, for him, she looked after a contagious woman and her diseased children in a hovel in Rome and stayed on to care for them. No other pilgrim did it. She reminded me of my good, artist friend, Irene, who had nursed till death an unknown Chinese sailor who had slipped through the welfare net, which regarded him as a nuisance. My friend Irene was a freethinker. So you didn't have to be labelled Christian to be Christian, and the converse is true. I didn't think I yet had the spiritual stamina but at least I learnt the price of entry into the kingdom of heaven.

But my real love remained the Saxon saints because I viewed the world as they did. A great darkness surrounded humankind. Waste places and dangerous marshes inhabited by monsters lay all around them. For them, those monsters were outer; for me at that time they were inner, but our situation was the same. Outside the storm raged, but a flickering candle of faith and goodness illumined our faces and was our protection against whatever the darkness could throw at us. Without that candle we were like the sparrow which winged its way from one darkness to another in the thane's hall. My darkness was the despair in me and the nightmares of the Holocaust behind me.

I was touched when I studied monuments and saw how other English people had stood up against the darkness of their time. I did not expect to be touched by Liverpool Cathedral. I have little liking for big buildings in modern medieval style. But in a side staircase there is a barred, stained glass window, recording modern women whose lives nourished me. One had told the poor and sick to wash their clothes in her boiler during the cholera epidemic. Another had gone down with a ship after seeing that everyone else got into the overcrowded lifeboats. Another, Josephine Butler, a real upper-class lady, had fought for the poor prostitutes of Liverpool against police brutality, nursing the syphilitic wrecks in the guest-rooms of her comfortable, respectable home. You can't get more godly than that. I think of her and her husband who supported her. They are what I came to love in England.

When I got back to Balliol I noticed a record to Adam vom Trott, an old boy who had been executed by Hitler. I also noticed the charred door recording the fire in which Cranmer and Ridley were martyred. In quantity, of course, the Holocaust dwarfed the sufferings of the Reformation – with its few hundred Protestant martyrs under Mary and the same number of Catholic martyrs under Edward and Elizabeth – but the quality of their courage and suffering was the same. My secular education had become a religious experience, a Christian one. At a time when I thought Jews were friendless and alone in their suffering, I recovered respect for my fellow human beings!

I felt at one with the countless pilgrims seeking the kingdom of heaven. Whether I had got to the kingdom of heaven I did not know. But I was now spiritually rooted in the United Kingdom, or one part of it.

10

I Read the Gospels

> The names in which men expressed their recognition
> of Him as such, Messiah, Son of Man, Son of God,
> have become for us historical parables. We can find
> no designation which expresses what He is for us . . .
> He will reveal Himself in the toils, the conflicts, the
> sufferings which they shall pass through in His
> fellowship, and, as an ineffable mystery, they shall
> learn through their own experience Who He is.
>
> Albert Schweitzer,
> *The Quest for the Historical Jesus*

After that extraordinary vacation, I summoned up my
courage and related my experiences to Christian friends
who were overjoyed – envious even. It seemed such
visitations weren't normal Christian life but rare plums,
which cheered me up. I was invited to very exclusive
ecclesiastical parties where plans for my impending
baptism were debated. I noted the subtle jockeying as to
who would have the honour of presenting me. Even if no
one wanted my body, at least they were all after my soul!
(I had a suspicion that with some of them my body might
come later!) I felt satisfied at being noticed by God above
and his creatures below and I licked my new spiritual
lips. One of the candidates for the honour of presenting

me gave me a New Testament to prepare myself – a book I'd overlooked in the excitement. It was like my Bar Mitzvah, my Jewish confirmation, all over again; same presents but different books. It would be a revelation, he said. But what it revealed was unexpected. I'd assumed that as I started reading it, I'd immediately bump into this being I'd met in the Quaker meeting but the being and the Gospels didn't match up, which left me disconcerted.

The Gospels were a puzzle, whether I tried to read them in pious bytes or in one go like a novel. A lot in them did touch me – the parables of the kingdom; Jesus himself, because he was a failure like me, but made something out of it which was hopeful; the Emmaus story; the fried-fish breakfast which ends the Gospels; the breathtaking opening of St John's Gospel; and the temptations in the wilderness. I didn't quite trust the last. Could he have really done what he was tempted to do? Probably not! So where was the choice? I cannot say I took to the Gospels as a whole, though I tried them first in English and then in a Hebrew translation.

I didn't know how to take them and on what level to trust them because I just couldn't believe in miracles. I tried. And if you took away the miracles from, say, Mark's Gospel, what was left? I didn't believe, for example, that whatever you asked your heavenly father for would happen – I'd been through that one before! At one time I thought I'd come near to believing quite a lot. But an atheist friend said I could test out my belief on him. We bet ten shillings (you could buy a lot with ten shillings in those days) on whether I could get near convincing him. I couldn't, and he kindly stood me lunch on his winnings. I could accept some of the psychosomatic healings, but noted that no one ever grew a new arm or leg, which might have made me sit up. Various people tried to bend my mind round the virgin birth or the disappearing body in the resurrection story, pointing out how fundamental the latter was for Paul – which was nice for Paul but got me nowhere. There was so much I couldn't cope with that it placed a question mark even over the bits I could.

I didn't exactly deny miracles because I'd never experienced one, but they just weren't part of my world. I've had the same problems with all Scriptures: Jewish, Christian or whatever.

I was a modern believer, which didn't make me a worse or better believer, but a different kind of believer. For my grandparents, the written Scripture was basic and they saw their lives as a commentary on it. '*Es ist geschrieb'n*' – 'so it is written' was the final seal of authority. For me and lots like me it isn't like that any more. Our basic text is our life experience, and all holy books are a commentary on that. Though getting a sensible commentary out of them is not easy because their subject matter is so long ago and far away. This role reversal of life and Scripture was a turning inside out I hadn't bargained for.

I remembered encountering this problem before. Though I learnt to read Hebrew as a child, I didn't learn to understand it. The prayer book was therefore for me a book of treasured wisdom beyond my comprehension. I watched old men swaying over it, kissing it, and putting their copies of it for safety and reverence in little velvet bags. At my Bar Mitzvah, I began to read the new English translation which was printed beside the Hebrew prayers, in a way that was never done in the older books. I was deeply disappointed. The prayers were so repetitious, not that interesting and loaded with compliments to the Almighty, telling him how wonderful he was. The music was nice, but I couldn't summon any enthusiasm for restoring the walls of Jerusalem (walls?) or setting up the throne of David (why?). It would have been better if I'd never understood it and allowed myself to imagine whatever I wanted.

The problem wasn't just in me but in the way religions use holy books. They set up false expectations. Books are meant to be read, whether they're illuminated Gospels or Torah scrolls. Instead, they are so idolised that any residual meaning is usually chanted away. I suppose that's the escape route for pious congregations, who otherwise might have the same impious thoughts as me. You don't have to understand a mantra, you just feel it.

This problem has never gone away. I had to spend most of my time as a minister trying to connect the Bible portions (already carefully selected) with any reality common to my congregation. Like most ministers, I got quite ingenious at it, but I kept on thinking that it was the wrong way round. We ought to start off with our reality and then work back to see if there was any guidance in the past. (Sometimes there was, sometimes there wasn't, and sometimes you could read into it whatever suited.)

I certainly couldn't connect up with the Gospel miracles. They lessened the religious meaning of the Gospels for me. If Jesus was human like me, then his life was relevant to me. If he was superman, raising the dead one minute and walking on the waters the next, then his life was curious but irrelevant. He signified only if he was ordinary. Wonders got in the way and there were even more of them in the New than in the Old Testament, and neither did him or me much good. They made our situation so different that it wasn't worth bridging the gap. And why were Christianity and Judaism so much nicer than their Scriptures, and their devotees nicer than the God they worshipped? Was God developing too, through his experience of his creatures, or was it just our perception of him that was developing? I tried to say this to some Christians at the time but they looked shocked.

The amount of anger in the Gospels shocked me. That poor blasted fig tree! Those poor porkers hurtling down the slope! Actually, I was pleased that the awkward bits were left in – it made me trust the other bits more. I could recognise Jesus, for example, as a touchy, Yid-disher, bright boy like me with the standard scenario of Jewish life – clever kid, shadowy, provider father, doting, doughty mother. His home situation was only too familiar.

But I didn't admire him much for producing showy miracles and then telling everyone around not to breathe a word about them to anybody. It showed a remarkable lack of insight into human nature or was a transparent device I'd used myself. Also a lot of the sayings sounded clever but weren't so clever on examination. 'Let the dead bury their dead' was good rhetoric but not good sense – because it was the living who were left with the arrangements. 'This is my body' could be taken whichever way. Some people liked their religion penny plain, some liked it tuppence coloured.

I stuck with the New Testament though, and found two problems went deeper than miracles. The exclusivity and extremism in the pages shook me morally. 'Many are called but few are chosen', 'the narrow gate', and so on. These didn't seem fair. Life was hard and to add cosmic insecurities to this world's insecurities seemed a dirty trick. Some Christians were really frightened of hell! Such a God I couldn't worship, whether he existed or not. Most Jews were more charitable to the Nazis than God was to those who crossed him, which was only too easy as he was very touchy. Marxism and Jewish communalism had led me in another direction, summarised neatly by Tom Lehrer, 'We'll all go together when we go.' That seemed compassionate! And if some of us had difficulty making it, then the others would have to help. That was what religion was about.

And such a fiery hell! Like cosmic concentration camps, divine Dachaus, blessed Belsens, sanctified Ravensbrucks! Worse, because there was no liberation ever, or release with death. I think Christians have got so used to it that they don't realise any longer what they are affirming. At first, I got worried whether I'd go to hell. Then I gathered enough courage to give it the old V-sign. I was insecure and paranoid but I still recognised what goodness was and I wasn't going to muddle it with sadism.

It was the exclusivity which I found the subtlest and most dangerous. Besides splitting people into sheep and goats, it also split the bits of both which coexist in all of us as well. The less ruthless pharisaic distinction between our good and evil inclinations, and the idea that both can be different sides of the same coin and feed into each other are more productive.

Rabbi Nachman ben Samuel taught that without the evil inclination people would not build houses, marry, have children or do business. He quoted, 'Work and skill both arise out of competition.'

I suppose the Pharisees thought of the evil inclination in a similar way to the Gospels – as power and ambition or sex. If you cut one of those evils out of a personality, that personality is not enriched but castrated. Such castration is heard in the floating, angelic voices of Christian liturgy and the fluting greetings of vicars. Such castration also leads to focusing the devil in you on somebody outside you and burning that somebody – like witches, Jews or gays – in order to get rid of it.

The extremism was also a turn-off. It didn't help me to reform. It just made me want to give up – like putting out your offending eye, or severing your naughty hand. You could either regard it as overblown religious rhetoric, in which case it could mean anything, or politely ignore it. The same thing applied to the couple who didn't give everything in the Acts of the Apostles (which I thought was only prudent) and were incinerated on the spot.

This wasn't like the smooth Catholicism (both varieties, Anglo- or Roman), or the gentle Quakers I knew. The thought world of the Gospels wasn't the gentle countryside inhabited by genteel residents in the cathedral closes of the west of England but the Wild West. The heirs of the Gospels must be the Pentecostals and Evangelicals who preached hellfire, judgment and damnation. Perhaps I ought to go to them! But common sense asserted itself. I would visit them but I wouldn't join up. I wasn't going to give myself over to anybody.

I tried to believe what I didn't. It was the same situation as I had been in with Marxism and there was really no point. I'd better remain a friendly outsider. Did I have enough material to put my own religion together? Yes, just enough, and in any case there was no other way. The Quakers or Unitarians suited me fine (I hadn't yet discovered progressive Judaism) because they also included in their ranks many refugees from traditional Christianity and Judaism. But neither felt like home. Unlike the Catholics I knew (both sorts), they were too good for me or I was too raffish for them. I preferred the company of sinners, provided they knew what they were. I also had a hankering at the time for mystery religions even though I never believed them. I am not proud of this low taste.

Many, many years later I met biblical scholars who tried to explain the Gospels in a different way. Things weren't what they seemed and you needed a lot of scholarship to discover what they were really trying to say. I'd heard the same story from Jewish scholars trying to justify every nook in the Old Testament too. I was reassured but decided no Scripture could ever be final for me. The one I wanted wasn't yet written and might never be. In the meantime I'd better set about piecing together my own provisional one. It would be poor and honest but my own.

11

The Dogmatic Skeleton

Many years after these tormented inner doubts and debates, when I had become a trainee rabbi, it became part of my job to marry people. I had to interview them, introduce them to the ceremonies, explain their meaning and what they were signing up to. The couples were too preoccupied to be more than polite, and I didn't blame them because they knew much more about the realities of the business than I did. The most important thing I asked them to consider was whether they meant the same thing by the words they recited to each other or signed up to. Many times they didn't, and their marriages later came unstuck in a fog of bewilderment and mutual recrimination.

I nearly made the same mistake myself, spiritually. Christianity was a love affair and I was going to marry myself to it through baptism. But the misgivings which followed my encounter with the Gospels made me examine the small print, its dogmas. Religious dogmas were something new to me. Judaism may or may not have them – it's still disputed – but I had never come up against them at religion classes. There, my curriculum consisted of practices, rituals, a bit of uncritical nationalist history and learning to read Hebrew fast – you got prizes for speed!

Christianity seemed closer to Marxism, where you also had to sign up to certain beliefs (like the infallibility of Uncle Joe) or got relegated by the Stalinists to outer darkness as a heretic or as a schismatic like Tito. But the universal Marxist doctrines were crystal clear and pedestrian compared to their cosmic Christian replacement.

Around the living flesh of the Jesus experience, there had grown up a hard, bony skeleton of structure. Even though I couldn't adhere to it in the end, I realised you couldn't base a life on experience alone. It might melt away on you just when you needed it.

So I grappled with orthodox Christian dogma and certainly got some amazing insights from it. But, as with Marxism, I could never swallow the whole package. I don't think many Christians could either but they were born to it.

This is what I got from gazing at the skeleton. At some date, mythic or actual, Adam and Eve whom God created (and who should have known better) did something to annoy him connected with nudity and sex. This was the Fall, which continued and continues in us till an immaculate virgin has a God-conceived child, whom human beings (especially Jews) murdered. This was a sacrifice whose death justified us to his father, our father. And if we human beings drink that blood which is now made from wine, we won't fall any more (or will we? I wasn't sure). Jesus is now a lamb in the form of a piece of consecrated Matzo (unleavened Passover bread) who takes away not only my sins but the sins of the world.

Somewhere in this structure, though in ways I couldn't understand, God revealed himself as One but in three persons, who knew it all before it all happened. Also, although hell was 'harrowed', heaven was for the few after a last judgment which would come sooner than we thought. Only God knew the names of those who would make it. But what did all this have to do with finding a friend inside me who released me from my own bitterness?

Now, I enjoy ideologies. They have the same fascination for me as bridge systems, which explains why I didn't stay with the Quakers who only had their 'inner light', which was too obvious. I probed instead different sorts of Catholicism and evangelical Protestantism, where stranger and stranger vistas unfolded that confused and titillated me. This was more fascinating than Marxism, and I began to see why Stalin had been a seminary student and the Fascist leaders such a pious lot.

But where did I stand in this drama of blood, guilt and cosmic reparation, this nightmare left over from the Apocalypse? Sometimes it seemed to make the profoundest sense; sometimes an inner madness focused on a cosmic screen. I think you have to be inside it to do it justice. To an outsider, it is only caricature. But all knowledge of God as it nears its centre can only be paradox.

I tried to approach it first in bits to see what I could make of them. Sometimes I could translate Christian doctrines into my own experience. As I was 'beside myself' at the time, I connected up with more than I expected. Sometimes the bits didn't connect up with any sense at all, though later on I met clerics and theologians who set them out with such subtlety that I wondered if I'd missed the point. But the following are the results of my Jewish, head-on approach at the time.

The key question for me was, 'Is Jesus "the way, the truth, the life" as far as my life is concerned?' He had certainly been a way to truth when I was very low. He had brought me to many truths and given me new life when I needed it badly. Perhaps he would do so again as

I approached the frontiers of life. But it was the exclusive bit which stuck in my throat. I had learnt other truths from analysis and therapy, which had saved me from suicide and the mental home, and some Marxist and anarchist truths stayed with me long after my defection. Later on, Vedanta truths were at work, making my partial truths coherent. Now orthodox Christianity affirmed that Jesus was *the* way, *the* truth, *the* life. I had to substitute 'a' for 'the'. I felt like a traitor at first but this was my truth.

The incarnation worried me less. The divine image lay deep inside every human being and those who worshipped the divine became like that which they worshipped. I recognised that image in the Jesus parables and stories, and then in other people, and lastly in myself. The gulf between the divine and creation, which cannot be bridged by common sense, can be bridged through ritual and in experience. It can also be bridged in acts of self-sacrifice and generosity. You know when it happens because heaven then feels very close.

The Trinity made sense when I imagined it as an electric current on the British loop system, which we can plug into at any point so that the current flows through us too. The chances and changes of life determine where we plug in. Another image helped me. I thought of two people I had watched in a station café. They were deeply in love and the love which flowed through them and united them was the third person of that trinity. The words of a song a novice sang also made sense: 'He's alive in you, and he's alive in me and the three of us together make a unity.'

I could adapt some beliefs to my life experience. Mary, for example, was 'my Yiddisher Momma', not the pretty doll of Christian iconography. Also, a Christian priest explained the Fall to me like this – we are imperfect people in an imperfect world, so do the best you can and don't let perfectionism make you give up. That certainly made sense, though was it Christian? It sounded rather Jewish to me!

Until I came up against Christian doctrine, I didn't realise how Jewish I was. An Anglo-Catholic friend sincerely congratulated me on my impending conversion. Jesus, he said, would save me from sin, death and hell. I was moved because he was moved for me, but I wasn't moved by his reasons. Like most Jews, I didn't believe in hell. In any case, I'd already gone through it or something like it on earth. I wasn't worried by death – only by the pain of dying – and psychotherapy with a retreat or two should get me out of my sins. I summoned up enough courage to tell him this and he told me sadly I was a Pelagian. I'd been called a Menshevik and a deviationist, so now I was a Pelagian. One day I'd look them all up.

It was the dark side of Christianity which was really the trouble. I didn't know what justification could mean. If it meant I was OK in the eyes of God that was fine, but that wasn't my worry. More important was wondering whether God was OK in my eyes because the world was a tough place. I'd been through a lot, and my family on the continent far, far more. I told this to the clergyman who might baptise me, and there was a long silence. He was nice enough afterwards but I knew and he knew, and I knew that he knew, that I was an outsider. As to faith and works, that was the chicken and egg problem. It was a matter of temperament whether you wanted to start at one end or the other.

Atonement for others interested me. It meant we could all draw on each other's spiritual bank accounts. I preferred this to sorting out the sheep and the goats. I was brought up to believe that you could ride piggyback on your teacher's piety and righteousness. This was a common tenet in Polish and Russian popular, Jewish mysticism.

Though I was not the 'believer' type, I really made an effort and was not unaffected by those Christian dogmas. They surfaced at unexpected times, at a party or during a committee meeting, for example, where I could see the Fall, or while watching two lovers in a café, as I've said, I could see the Trinity in action.

Judaism is a family, though often a big, unhappy one. Whatever keeps quarrelling families together keeps us together too. But Christianity was not like that. It might have been an experience once but it was now a belief system, a set of doctrines, a church.

As to the Scriptures, I read them again and it seemed to me all our Scriptures were incomplete, Jewish and Christian. Neither the Old Testament, nor the New Testament, nor the Talmud, for example, called for an end to slavery, only for its amelioration. Yet that was the real evil of Jesus's time. Spartacus had seen the problem more clearly – I was at one with the Marxists on that. It took centuries of Jewish and Christian life-experience before they came to the same conclusion, though, according to Simone Weil, an unknown Greek philosopher long before Plato had seen the institution itself as evil. The Holy Spirit had a lot of work to do in the meantime. Thank God that Spirit is working in us now to complete the Scriptures. If we deify holy books, they become a cage, not a call to progress. And cages can be wicked things.

Sitting in the theology library, I realised at long last that the rows of books could not get me where I wanted.

The Dogmatic Skeleton

I needed to meet Christians, real live ones, before I knew
if their world was mine. Also, I needed to compare notes.
Were most Christians as muddled as me?

12

Christian Lives

So I set out to see Christianity from another angle – not from Scriptures or books of doctrine but cooked in people's lives. After all, my own experience had not come from any book or Gospel but from my own need. So perhaps I'd come closer to the Jesus I'd met incarnated in people's life-experience. I'd go on a church crawl, much more interesting and relevant than a boozy, Oxford, pub crawl.

I did stumble across Jesus in other people's lives but not in places of power. This is because the only power that God has in the world is the love he inspires in us. Otherwise he would have released the victims of the Nazis from their hell. But *Fidelio* is opera, not reality.

So I responded to Christianity where it didn't put on the style. I remember a service of the Metropolitan Community Church held in a hired hall. Unless you're lesbian or gay, you may not have heard of such a church because that's whom it primarily caters for. It's not allowed a seat on the World Council of Churches, for example. But then I wasn't interested in seats on councils, only in people who had shared my experience and could tell me more about it.

Their liturgy was a curious goulash of all the traditions the members had had to leave behind. Like the gypsy stew in *The Wind in the Willows*, it had bits of everything in it. There were Eastern Orthodox bits, Catholic and Anglican bits, Plymouth Brethren bits, Free Church bits and Halleluiah bits. The kiss of peace was great stuff, and someone pressed his knee companionably against mine, though not as a pick-up because he was quite well suited.

What got under my skin was their humility. My visit was not many years after the beginning of gay liberation, so they'd had difficult lives. Some had obviously suffered from breakdown. But as with me, Jesus had turned their world inside out too and they genuinely tried to love each other. Over tea and coffee after the service, I told myself, 'This is the gate of heaven', and it was. They had straight members, too, they told me proudly; other bed-sitter folk and old people who didn't feel marginalised or patronised in such a congregation. Like the early Christians they were rejects from the establishment.

I was also touched by a visit to the home of the Hebrew Christian Alliance, which I had made out of curiosity, not because of their evangelical theology. An old woman, who reminded me of my grandmother, who would have held up her hands in horror, told me tranquilly how she had kept her faith when she was rejected not only by Nazis and Jews but also by her own church. She was Lutheran of Jewish parents. I couldn't have endured so many rejections. But she incarnated what she believed in. I was interested in her inner strength.

Later, when my parents sent me to Israel to be 'koshered' again, I met a poor, unsuccessful evangelist, wandering dazedly through the streets of Jewish Jerusalem. Not the glitzy kind, of course, and his congregation consisted of two families, a lunatic and me. I never attended to his proof texts and tortured commentary, but I was touched by him and his muddled 'call'. I hoped he would never inherit the earth because he would make such a mess of it. Or would he? What are success and failure when they're inside out? Anyway, I used to escort him home and steer him away from causing a riot. Years later, I listened to rehearsed and successful evangelists. When they invited converts to make themselves known and be led down the aisles, I sat stolidly in my seat munching toffees.

I recognised other people who had had an experience like mine. There was a friar in a priory who conscientiously collected the garbage left by visitors. Other friars did too, when they could be bothered. But he did it with love because Jesus was beside him. You could spot the difference. As a Jewish devotee once said, 'I don't go to my rabbi to learn Scripture but to watch the way he ties his shoes!'

And there was a French chap in a gay sauna who used to cuddle and kiss the rejected old men there. (Sex can be predatory and selfish.) Did he like old men? I asked curiously. They were not a particular turn on for him, he said, considering my question, 'though they are for some', but that's what Jesus wanted of him. I understood. Redeemers are most needed in a meat market. That was his call.

There was also a priest I met in a hedgerow while hitch-hiking to the Med. He wanted to say Mass in the field and asked me to serve for him. I told him my peculiar Christian situation but this didn't seem to bother him and he even asked me if I'd like to take communion. The wafer, he said, wasn't a prize for good behaviour or right thoughts but a help to them. I said yes and did take the wafer. I felt moved, but it didn't 'take' in the sense that I needed it again or couldn't lead my religious life without it. What moved me was his generosity because I sensed how much it meant to him. I once asked a cabbalist rabbi what religion was really about and his answer surprised me: 'The art,' he said, 'of giving without strings.' My hedgerow priest gave without strings and this I have never forgotten. Whether or how Jesus was in the wafer I do not know, but he certainly lived in the generosity of that priest. That was another manifestation to ponder over in the long intervals between lifts.

The Christian service I remember most was a worldly failure. I had missed my train at Euston and went over to Friends House for the Quaker service to while away the time. Just after the chairman opened the meeting a man rushed in from the street and began to testify, telling the congregation how he had been defrauded by the government, parliament, monarchy, banks and traitorous friends. It was a clear case of paranoia. He went on like that for nearly forty minutes while the congregation listened silently with closed eyes. Then his ranting ended, and the chairman closed the meeting for there was no more time. All who had attended lined up and courteously thanked him for his grisly testimony. He went out mollified and mumbling into the street. Their politeness was spiritual uncommon sense, another case of 'turning inside out', and I have never forgotten it or ceased to be moved by the memory.

I had a homely love affair with Christianity. It was like a spiritual box of chocolates – there were so many delicious things in it – Anglican evensong and compline in country parish churches; the dawn breaking through the windows of monastery chapels during the long morning silence and feeling the rebirth of creation; the non-Christmas parties some generous Sisters of Sion made for their Jewish friends in December because they didn't want them to feel left out; the surprise of seeing the way, the truth, the life in unexpected people, whose generosity passed my understanding.

But I also noticed that the power of Christianity, from which it derives its strength, is not worldly and outer but is the power of love, and inner. Those meetings, congregations and churches to which I was so drawn had not fallen for worldly temptation. I suppose they were never offered the chance! And they didn't put on the style because they couldn't afford it. They had their temptations too, of course, because 'whenever two or three are gathered together in my name' you can be pretty sure one becomes chairman, another secretary and another treasurer. But I was privileged to experience them at their 'incompetent' best.

I did get glimpses of the other side. I shall never forget watching a hundred professional priests and students marching as to war in full fig, bearing aloft crosses while organs boomed and choirs let loose. I was the only Jew there, and one member of the procession gazed at me triumphantly. This was the works, he seemed to say. But all it reminded me of was the brute force of the Roman legions. Like the interior of St Peter's in Rome, that procession was a turn-off.

My tranced wander around things Christian came to an abrupt end when I informed my mother over the telephone that she might have to think of me henceforth as 'my son, the Christian'. I had had enough of not belonging anywhere. To sugar the pill, I told her I might even become a bishop or canon, living in a nice Laura Ashley close. Most Jewish mothers like success.

My mother didn't mince her words. If I became a Christian monk, she said, she would commit suicide and my father too. She was just having her change of life, she

added, and would hold me responsible for the consequences. She rang off, leaving the phone off the hook to
make sure I was left holding the baby!

I decided to test out the strength of my new faith,
dropped into an Anglo-Catholic church and asked to see
a priest. I must have interrupted his dinner because he
was short with me. There was no problem, he said. I had
to leave my mother and father, dead or alive; that's what
it said in the Gospels. (I later checked it up and he was
right.)

'No more?' I asked, taken aback, expecting a plangent
examination of my call and conscience.

'No more!' he reiterated, and scuttled back to dinner,
leaving me in the darkening church with some hard
choices to meditate over.

I got on my knees and consulted my Jesus, who said,
'Balls!' He liked my father and mother and I had caused
her quite enough trouble during her change of life. Who
did I believe, him or the priest? Or neither?

I certainly didn't believe anybody enough to murder
my parents. I couldn't do the dirt on them like that. I
didn't believe enough to let any church take me over.
That wasn't inside out, that was just the wrong way up!

13

A Second Experience

I didn't fall into the font for many reasons, my mother's threat being merely one of them. To be honest, I didn't take it that seriously. Like me, she was a survivor, not a martyr-type. She thought all official religion a luxury, not meant for working women like her but for women with afternoons free for bridge and good works. Like many Jews, she was also inclined to hyperbole. In any case, part of me shared her doubts. Of course, I had lots of doubts about Judaism too, and so did she if she thought about it, which she didn't. But that was different because we were born into it and took it as a package deal.

The main reason I didn't jump into the baptismal font was another experience, as nasty as the first one was nice, but none the less real.

Dear Christian reader,

I'm going to put this in the form of a letter because what I'm going to say might hurt you – will hurt you – and I'm sorry, really sorry, because you've given me so much. I feel close to you and there's a lot I share with you.

This second experience happened during Lent 1951 in a church. I was forlornly tramping round it, following in the wake of a bedraggled procession who were doing the stations of the cross. I then sat listening to the readers in a vigil, occasionally dipping into those Gospels my friends had given me, when a wave of pent-up anger surged up in me and nearly drowned me in my own fury. I could hardly hold the book because I was trembling so much. Anger at the church I sat in, anger at the Gospels in my hand, anger against this appalling Christianity which had been responsible for so much murder. 'His blood be upon us and upon our children!' (Matthew 27:25). The author could congratulate himself on a dramatic success, because the letters of the text in my hand dripped with the blood of persecutions, pogroms and burnings.

I thought of the way that murderous anti-Judaism had fed into Hitler's anti-Semitism. I wanted to retch as I saw the cattle trucks with their human cargoes of misery on their way to the camps, where sentimental guards sang 'Silent Night' at Christmas. I thought about DeValera sending condolences to the German Ambassador over Hitler's death, the Nazi-Christian Evangelical theologians, Pius XII too neutral to mention the gas chambers, how decent people like my own family were turned into devils by crude Christianity (I'd experienced that at school).

I thought of such Christian inventions as the ghetto and the Jewish badge of shame. The Nazis didn't have to go very far to pick up their know-how. I thought of the dirges sung in synagogues commemorating our expulsion from Spain, to which we'd given so much; of the innocent left on sandbanks to drown or sold into slavery. It was too much, too much, and I burst into tears not out of Christian piety as my neighbours thought but out of anti-Christian anger. How could I ever think of joining them after the Holocaust? How could I ever betray our terrible Jewish history under them? Where was all that vaunted love and kindness in this:

A synagogue is less honorable than any inn. For it is
not simply a gathering place for thieves and huck-
sters, but also of demons. Indeed, not only the
synagogue, but the souls of Jews are also the dwelling place of demons.

St John Chrysostom

or in this:

You have slain your Lord in the midst of Jerusalem . . . He who hung the earth in its place is hanged,
he who fixes the heavens is fixed upon the cross . . .
the Master has been insulted, God has been
murdered, the King of Israel has been slain by an
Israelite hand.

Bishop Melito, second century

Discrimination against Jews can be read in Thomas
Aquinas, and insults against Jews in Martin Luther.

I looked around. Here they all were, in this very church,
after our six million died, unconsciously sowing the seeds
of horror again. I wanted to shout out but didn't dare.

And this Christian poison hasn't stopped yet. Later on,
in Spain, I knocked on the doors of a convent to join the
enclosed nuns in their early morning prayer. The nun
porteress told me the sisters were on retreat, but before
I left she called me back out of compassion and handed
me through the grille a small pamphlet as consolation. It
was another wicked 'testimony' to the blood libel!

After that I ventured again into a London church at
Eastertime. The priest, a pleasant old man, had still
retained those awful anti-Jewish recriminations in the
liturgy. Then, during 'the peace', he recognised me and

came towards me with compassion and forgiveness written all over his face. I didn't feel like forgiving him. I don't risk Easter any more.

Apart from all this Gospel stuff, Christianity was an even worse persecutor of sex – my sex – than even Judaism (which lied to itself by denying that such Jews as me existed). I despised myself for thinking of joining my persecutors. I felt like one of the 'trusty' Jewish police in the ghettos, who got a special deal for a while by sucking up to their Nazi tormentors.

But during that Lenten vigil, no one seemed aware of the hidden sadism, masochism and murder all around. I looked up at the statues and pictures. Tortures everywhere! Didn't they realise how kinky it all was? – like the bondage and blood in sex shops. No wonder they burnt anyone who disagreed with them. They were trying to burn away their own suppressed sex and unacknowledged doubt.

I left the church and retched into a nearby loo. I knew I would never be baptised, or ever become a card-carrying Christian. The Holocaust lay between me and them like a black cloud, a corpse, a dead weight.

What was the origin of all this pious dirt? I suppose it's so much easier making your own faith nicer by diabolising others. The more villainous the Pharisees, the sweeter Jesus appears. And Jews practise it too. The more you diabolise Paul, the politer Jews become about Jesus. The more you run down the mother goddess, the more you can make of the prophets.

Why am I speaking with such raw passion about people of long ago? Because, like most Jewish children, during the evacuation I was called a Christ-killer and was punished with a punch-up in the playground.

Here endeth my epistle to the Christians!

A Second Experience

Later, a long time later, when I had recovered from this anger, I knew this couldn't be the end of the matter. What about that experience in the Quaker meeting? That inner conversation had entered into me and become part of me. I couldn't deny that either. It would be a spiritual castration. But how to put together the love that surged up in me then and the anger that overwhelmed me now?

Bits of an answer, eliptic bits, did come but not suddenly. They came from musing on a saint, an unofficial one. I had always been curious about saints since I first encountered them in Bede. I wanted to observe how God had fused himself into people's lives.

I do not remember how I first came across the name of Franz Jäggerstätter, because he was hardly known in the fifties. Probably it was through some article in a pious magazine. Like many saints he wasn't an 'important' person – just an Austrian burger in a provincial town who, when he got his call-up papers to Hitler's army, had a long think, decided he could not in conscience comply and sent them back. He knew this wasn't a defensive, holy war. He'd seen the obvious.

No one wanted to punish him and they all tried to make it easy for him to comply – officials, his wife, his bishop – but he couldn't. Unlike the great and good, he recognised the obvious. It wasn't right. He said so, and was beheaded in 1943. Just one simple death among so many deaths, and not the worst either, but it showed up so many people who should have known better. I suppose that's why he's never made it for canonisation yet – still a bit too hot to handle!

I was about to become angry all over again when I saw my anger turn inside out, because it showed me up, too. I had a think. What would we religious Jews have done if

Hitler had beheaded only Commies and tortured homos, leaving respectable Jews like us alone? How many of us would have complied to save our skins? Some would have said it was for the sake of our congregations. Others would have gone further and said that though Hitler was a bit extreme, something had to be done about such riff-raff.

But then the question progressed and it became a boomerang when it pointed at me. What would I have done if I'd been put to the test? Would I have risked my own life for people I hardly knew, like Franz Jäggerstätter? Perhaps I would. Who knows? More probably, I would have looked the other way at best or become another apologist for evil at worst. And my sin would have even been worse, being a closet homo who should have known better.

I remembered a childhood incident I had hidden in the recesses of my mind. In the thirties, when the Fascists were marching through London's East End and my mother pushed me into a shop doorway to hide, I rebelled inwardly. I longed for a drum and a black shirt to march with them – even though they were throwing Jewish oldies through shop windows and terrorising people. I didn't want to be on the losing side any more. I was fed up with Jewish weakness, timidity and fear, with being on the losing side. I didn't want any more Jewish senti-mentality and Jewish suffering. I was sickened by our sad songs. If only I could have changed sides. Thank God, I couldn't!

> Has none a fist and where's a thunderbolt
> to take revenge for all the generations
> to tear the world and blast the heavens asunder
> and wreck the universe My throne of glory!

These lines were written by the early Zionist poet, Bialick. I felt the same!

But our Jewish God didn't get off scot-free either. The world he created, if he did, wasn't a pretty place. I got acquainted with it in 'All things bright and beautiful' that I sang at school, or the 'O God, you're wonderful, marvellous, so powerful, so bossy, so self-righteous' stuff they taught us as children at Hebrew and religion classes. The whole house of cards came crashing down. 'You're only a pack of cards,' said Alice. I said something crude, rude and basic to both the Christian God and the Jewish God together.

As I remembered the honest, crude temptations of long ago, I winced. The self-righteousness oozed out of me. I was on the same level as the church. We were birds of a feather. So to change, to convert? Why bother!

14

No-Man's-Land

This second experience sent me into a deep depression which only began to disperse after I left England and religion itself – all brands. Once again I was homeless. I had no physical friend and all my sublimation substitutes had cracked up. Christianity had gone the same way as traditional Judaism, anarchism and Marxism.

I remembered from my childhood others whose homelessness used to make me shiver. They were the few Jews who had deserted to the other side and become Christian converts. I remembered the silence that fell over our little street as one of them passed by, how I had to avert my eyes from them and how their pamphlets were consigned to the fire or the dustbin. Many would only touch them with tongs. I also had to avert my eyes from the pictures in the local, medical, Christian mission to the Jews too, when poverty and illness forced us through its doors. I had to wash my mouth out afterwards if I was persuaded into saying a prayer there.

I was fascinated by those exiles from the warmth of Jewish family and community who were neither one thing nor the other, but lived in a desolate no-man's-land which separated pious little Judaism from the overweening power and pomp of the church. I was now in an even more parlous case than them because I wasn't even Christian.

Free from all religion, I now saw clearly that though the traditional religions talked about love, they had never really loved each other. They didn't even know each other, only their own misunderstanding of each other. Of course, they couldn't admit they didn't love each other but their past hostilities and persecutions were proof enough. They regarded each other like modern multinationals, beadily and calculatedly, competing not for consumers but for souls. It was interesting how fulsome they were about the statistics of those who had joined up, but they were more economical about the number of those who had left. From this harsh judgment I except fringe groups who had never been seduced by power or the numbers game, such as Quakers, Bahai or Hindu Vedantists.

The no-man's-lands which separate all faiths are not pleasant places. I had seen *All Quiet on the Western Front* at the pictures and I likened them to the eerie trenches in Flanders fields. And the most desolate of them all was the no-man's-land which separated Judaism from Christianity. It must have started out as a family quarrel (those are always the worst) which turned nasty with charges of deicide, schism, apostasy, treachery and desertion. The secular power was then called in to accomplish by force what could not be accomplished by love or reason. This had led to the Inquisition and ghettos. In modern times this anti-Judaism had fed into anti-Semitism, out of which came the gas chambers and the camps. Mentally, I know it takes two to tango and there must be a Christian side as well, but being conditioned by my environment, as Marx said, I didn't see it. That was my limitation.

Even as a child it was a puzzle. How did I put together the pogroms in my grandmother's memory, the flaming flesh of Jewish history, with the 'gentle Jesus meek and mild' of school prayers? As an adult, how could I reconcile such horrors with the Christian love and friendship offered to me at Oxford in 1950 and since?

Now I too had to build a makeshift home in no-man's-land. Originally I thought I was the only one in no-man's-land but this was my delusion. I was like the solitary rider on the horizon described by Stephen Leacock, who was joined by another solitary rider and yet another until the horizon was crowded with solitary riders. To my surprise, this 'blasted heath' was more inhabited than I thought. I met doubters and converts pushing their way across in both directions, a few honoured for their sincerity, most rejected as traitors for their disloyalty. Penetrating into it even further, I was astonished by the nobility of the Christian converts to Judaism in the Middle Ages and under the Nazis, when both converter and convert could be, and were, burnt at the stake, or worse. And I now understood those Jewish converts to Christianity whom my parents tried to hide from me, lest they cast their spell over me. How difficult such journeys must have been for all of them, in a time of rising modern racialism.

Later, I discerned other travellers in the smoke of combative theology which hung over no-man's-land. I stumbled over the honest scholars more interested in truth than apologetics, the Reuchlins of the Renaissance, the Leo Baecks of modern times. They got little thanks, trying to be impartial in a war zone, amid the exploding salvos of propaganda and counter-propaganda which are called apologetics. I was especially drawn to the outsiders, the rag-tag and bobtail of all religions and none, seeking for bits of answers anywhere. A few were nutters, and some were visionaries, but together they were my sort of people. I honoured them because they weren't cocksure of themselves and their limited belief system.

Many years later, I was so happy when I met many of them again among the listeners to my sermonettes and God-slots on the BBC. It was such a relief talking to searchers and not card-carrying, committed believers. I wanted to kiss them through the mike.

Eventually I got to like no-man's-land. And God must have liked it too, because he was more present to me there than in any place of pious pilgrimage. I learnt a lot about love in no-man's-land – not cupboard-love but the real sort – and it lasted longer than any other kind.

Teresa of Avila – for whom I have high, though qualified, regard – says that if there are two ways in front of you, choose the harder, because spiritually speaking it will be the more profitable. Most prophets, seers and humble seekers have retired into a desert at some time in their lives. I don't think you can get very far without paying one a visit, whether you call it a desert or wasteland or no-man's-land. Where else do you learn to see the truth without illusion, and give role-playing a rest? Where else can you get in touch with your own religion – not other people's? Where else do you love the truth for its own sake, and God too, because he is truth?

15

When Your Religion Goes Wrong

Yet I am here a chosen sample,
To show Thy grace is great and ample;
I'm here a pillar o' Thy temple
    Strong as a rock,
A guide, a buckler, and example,
      To a' Thy flock.
          From 'Auld Willie's Prayer',
              Robert Burns

In no-man's-land you can see clearly, because there's no need for special pleading or pretending that everything in your ecclesiastical patch is lovely. You don't have to apologise any more or role-play or over-assert yourself. It's no longer your job to prop up an establishment or defend a dodgy tradition or gloss over feelings and faults.

Pilgrim's Progress has been my life's companion, but I had to accept that Bunyan's views on poor old women as witches was dreadful and the Quakers whom he fought against were right. He was also responsible for a very nasty sermon on limbo and its poor inhabitants. Jews, who have been a humane and constructive element in societies which never appreciated them, still did their share of slave-trading both in medieval Bristol and in colonial times, just like Christians – like everybody in fact except Quakers.

If you have only lived in one religion, you can never see its problems – you are too much of an insider. If you have lived in two or more, you cannot help seeing the same pattern of problems in all of them though they wear different guises. The divisions between liberal and reform Jews looked remarkably like those between ritualists and modernists in the C. of E. Orthodox, Conservative, Reform, Liberal were all Christian labels transferred to Judaism. When I returned to Judaism from Christianity, I had a sense of déjà vu. Christianity taught me a lot about the problems of Judaism. It didn't intend to. It was a lesson in negative, not positive, truth but it saved me from deep blasphemies against the spirit. The good Lord may be smiling wryly above, but such insight was one of the greatest gifts of Christianity to me.

As I list the following illnesses of religion it may be helpful to keep a ballpoint at your side to mark off all the ones that apply to you. It is distressing reading, but accepting the difficult truth is the mark of true humility. Religion is not only kind and generous. It also has its dark side. Believers have burnt, beheaded and tortured unbelievers and other believers. Being religious is, alas, not enough. It has to be the right religion, good religion, the first-class stuff. Any other can be very dangerous.

Many illnesses of religion are the result of unrealistic expectations. We are supposed 'to love God with all our heart and all our soul and all our might', which is a tall order, well-nigh impossible, considering the abyss between us. You can certainly try, knowing that you will fail, though the words seem absolute and not for compromisers. These are some of the short cuts that seduce believers like us, faced with such an unearthly expectation.

One short cut is to make God small, to bring him down to your size. Since he is so high above, you can't grow up enough in love and generosity to reach him, so why not take a short cut and reduce him to your height instead? That way, religion becomes manageable – cosy even. He becomes the God of your little group, your class, your church, your nation. He is your totem, the God of John Betjeman's lady, worshipping in wartime Westminster Abbey, the God of Burns' Auld Willie. He is the God of all nationalism (Jewish included). He is the Lord of your self-interest. For your spiritual growth, he is dangerous because you start to worship your own limitations.

It is not enough to be generous and unselfish yourself. You have to make sure your religion is generous and unselfish too. Otherwise you become nicer than your religion or the God you worship. Unfortunately, people are brought up to believe that the fault is never in their faith, which is sacrosanct by definition, but only in themselves. This is why such saintly, good people do so much harm in Israel, Palestine, Northern Ireland and Burma.

Another way to reduce God to size is much less premeditated. In fact it is usually unconscious and you only notice this device in yourself and others if you have experienced two or three faiths, as I have indicated.

In my situation it would go like this. 'To believe like me, you would have to become like me, to dress like me, live like me, love like me, inhabit the same suburb as me – in other words be me or my clone!' This is the logic of much missionary work – both Christian and Jewish – and though not a sin, it is a mistake. It also leads to the diminution of God and the worship of your own milieu. Respectability takes the place of religion.

There is another way of growing in piety, which is more dangerous for all concerned, much more dangerous than the two I've mentioned. That is increasing love for your own by decreasing love for outsiders. In its simplest form it can be witnessed on children's playgrounds. A group of children tighten their bond of friendship by banding against another child outside their circle. Since the aim of religion – especially Christianity, according to its self-proclaimed intention – is universal love, this provides a short-term advance by mortgaging your future religious development. You've blocked your own path to universal love. This is very serious for Jews and all ethnic religious groups, who withdraw their love from outsiders to increase their love for insiders. It is in fact a temptation to all 'elect' or 'chosen' or 'infallible' groups or sects. They forget that God is in their opponents too.

This is so important that I shall try to explain it again. A baby starts off by loving itself. It then proceeds to love its mother and its family, if life has been kind to it. Then its love stretches out further to love those who love it, its group, its community, its nationality. All these widening circles of love and respect are right in themselves, and a preparation for greater religious love, when you try to love people who do not love you, even your competitor, your adversary, your enemy. The temptation is to arrest your development at one stage, and never get beyond loving your own by diabolising the outsider. Comparative religion, often regarded as an enemy, helped to save me from this, which is a characteristic of all fundamentalism.

You can see this happening on a children's playground. You can also see it in Northern Ireland, in the Holy Land, in every quarter of the globe, in me and, if you are perceptive, in you too.

When Your Religion Goes Wrong

Religions, like individuals, have their own psychological make-up. When things go wrong they incline to different weaknesses, different neurotic or psychotic patterns. Judaism, my home religion, uses compulsive neurosis to cope with insecurity, just as I did as a child, instructed by my holy, anxiety-ridden grandmother. Instead of not treading on cracks between paving-stones or touching things, its ritual compulsions are more sophisticated, like going back to the beginning of a prayer if you make a tiny mistake, or making major fusses about minor pieties. So Jewish life is agog with communal dramas, like worrying about the glue on postage stamps, or which kiss-proof lipstick is kosher, or touching menstruant women (wear gloves!), and countless other curious practices. These are mostly harmless, except to those who take this pious cat's-cradle too seriously and are too entwined to ask for their deeper meaning. Convents suffered from them too. It is a symptom of a deeper anxiety, too frightening to face.

Christianity falls for another neurosis. This became immediate to me when I went on my first 'church crawl' in Oxford. It is not immediate to most Christians because they are so used to it that they do not see it. It is sado-masochism. Images of torture are present everywhere in crucifixions, flaying, floggings, burnings – enough to rate as kinky as if they were in a sex shop. (There are non-violent images, too, but they're not so visible, such as the Good Shepherd, nativities, St Jerome reading. These are scarce.) I do not think this obsession was always there. In Romanesque iconography, Jesus is a pleasant country lad and Mary and Joseph solid peasant folk. It is when everything gets elongated and weird and Gothic that the creepiness comes in. Christianity has never been happy about sex. 'It is better to marry than to burn' is no basis for marriage. And with so much suppressed sex around no wonder asexual heretics and Jews were suspected of strange sexual deviations. The deviations were not in the heretics or Jews but in the minds of the Christians who burnt them.

The fruits of such a deviation are also obvious in Christian history. No other religion has burnt so many heretics, has spilt so much blood over doctrines more easily remembered than understood. Why this neurotic pattern should be there I do not understand. But it certainly produces enormous guilt and fear. Mixed with much genuine love, the result is both fascinating and fearsome.

There is one modern fault all religions share – whether traditional or progressive. We live in a materialist age and this materialism rubs off on religion too. But the Holy Spirit, the Holy Ghost, 'Old Smoky' is not material. He is very, very see-through, and you can only sense his presence by faith. This is not good enough, and all of us would like to materialise him a little more. We want materialist evidence for what is not material. So in Catholic Christianity, St Bernardettes dance, and Virgin Marys weep, and those who see these goings on rightly rub their eyes in amazement, and the official church keeps mum. These manifestations don't do much harm except in disguising doubt as faith.

In my own Judaism, a similar reversion to holy places has been more dangerous. Jerusalem was not known personally to my East European forebears, who honoured it and fantasised about it at a safe distance. None of the great rabbis who had formed their faith had ever visited it, such as Rashi, the Vilner Gaon, or the Baal Shem Tov. They would have done if they had thought their faith depended on it.

In recent times with the coming of Zionism, Jerusalem has become a centre for pious tourism, much favoured by Americans who like solid objects and have a religious building mania. But unfortunately it doesn't stop there. Jerusalem became a holy city and then a political holy city and then a cause of riots and confrontations. And soon it may end in murder and disaster. My teacher told me that the Bible does not talk of holy cities, only of cities of holiness – cities where holy actions have been done. That is far safer. Holy cities are very dangerous, especially for secular believers. Holy deeds are what is needed. I was surprised at how much Jerusalem meant to Jesus, considering how it was sidelined later on by Rome and Constantinople.

The materialism, by the way, does not only concern what is above the surface. After all, the biblical city of Jerusalem lies far beneath the present surface. So inspired archaeologists have begun to burrow, hoping to find God knows what under the old foundations – perhaps God! Of course this is interesting, but it has led to more riots and though relevant to early history it is not important for theology. To find God now, you have to burrow within, not below.

I suspect all religions have their favoured neurotic fault lines where they are likely to go wrong. However, I do not know many as intimately as I know Christianity and Judaism, so I can only guess what they are. I suspect that when Islam goes off course it descends into megalomania. You question something and the answer is a text. You question the text and the answer is another text. All the answers are there but as the reality of Islamic states and republics is not at present prepossessing, the reality doesn't fit the answers. Jews and Christians suffer from megalomania too. They do not want to know what they don't know, which is difficult. They prefer to know it all, like God, which is easy. Then bossiness replaces listening and everybody knows exactly what is right for everybody else. Pious Taleban males in Afghanistan know just what is right for Afghan females, and everybody knows who the holy places belong to – themselves, naturally! Heterosexuals know just what is right for homosexuals, just as a Jewish waiter at a banquet told me exactly what food was fit for me to eat. I had to point out that I was the rabbi there, not him. It is so easy to identify with the God we worship, to feel that we have to defend him from his own creation. This bossiness comes up most in fundamentalists.

But I do not wish to be partisan about the illnesses of religion. Every party has its own. In the progressive part of Judaism, religion is very easily hijacked by the Zeitgeist, respectability, and by any fashion that comes to hand at the time. It has little protection against the cult of worldly success and failure. It also has difficulty in coping with the hard bits of religion, the parts which involve giving up.

A less showy mistake is made by the orthodox of all faiths – the worship of tradition in its own right. Tradition is and has been a way to God and often the most well-trodden, but it is not God. This is difficult to spot because it seems so pious, but the end is a mummification of the living word, a glorification of a romantic past that never was – in Judaism a kind of Jewish Confucianism. It is actually a way of killing the living God stone dead by smothering him in holy wrappings.

Ritual chanting is an expression of this. The tune and the atmospherics kill the words underneath them – perhaps that is their unacknowledged purpose. This is appropriate in a bhakti form of devotion, centring on love, but it feels wrong for a religion like Judaism working in the world for the righteous and holy society. It can serve as another opium for the masses.

I want to end this doleful list with the most dangerous illness of all. Religious people can be so eager to convert others to their truth that they get exasperated by how those foolish others cannot see what is to obvious to them. So they are tempted by the most devilish short cut of all – why not cut through the Gordian knot of explanation and force others to see their truth? That is when they invoke the powers of the state. There is even a bonus in this method. In doing so they can make political power spiritual. How can God not approve? But he doesn't because instead of spiritualising politics, the people themselves become politicised. And people whose consciences are forced learn how to dissemble and how to hate.

These are some of the truths I learnt from being Jewish Orthodox, Marxist, Christian, Vedantist and Jewish Reform. They are not pleasant truths but they made me suspicious of specious nonsense and I remain grateful to all of them whatever their view of me.

Many centuries ago, the rabbis pointed out that higher animals decompose more quickly than lower ones. It is because Christianity aims at such dizzy spiritual heights (and sometimes almost achieves it) that it can also descend so low in nit-picking nastiness. I glimpsed both – I had a ringside seat. I learnt from both. The depths too were a valuable revelation – the warning kind – and I learnt to see what was in front of my eyes in the harsh light of no-man's-land.

16

The Naked Truth

And all must love the human form
in heathen, Turk or Jew.
Where Mercy, Love and Pity dwell,
there God is dwelling too.

William Blake

After my blinding anger in the church and the depression
that followed, I decided I was too neurotic for religion. I
wanted no angels, no divine beings, no sublimation with
see-through lovers. I would concentrate on the things of
this world instead, on my poor matter-of-fact body, my
poor, poor body that my soul and mind had ganged up
on. I had found out I could do just that in Amsterdam,
Europe's own Greenwich Village. So I nervously sang a
different 'Song of Ascents' as I took a ticket on a clanking
tram outside Amsterdam Station. Someone had passed
me the address of a heaven you could get to by public
transport.

The tram passed through the tourist streets I knew,
and I got off uneasily in a shabby working-class district
which reminded me of my London childhood. A few
streets from the tram stop I rang the bell of an incon-
spicuous sauna and met Tina, my big-hearted, big-
bosomed, blonde Tina, who persuaded me to undress

though I was frozen by shyness, replacing my heavy clothes with an inadequate towel which couldn't be made to meet around my middle. She comforted me with coffee and cookies before gently pushing me through a door into the cosy darkness of her sauna for 'mature men'. She said I could tell her all about it afterwards.

Gay people were used to being despised and rejected at that time, even by the café owners and waiters who made money out of them. But Tina was punctilious about our dignity. Surnames were never mentioned but titles were. So it was *Mijnheer* this and Dominee or Doctor that, and they could fill in the rest for themselves if they wished.

At about ten to four she knocked at the door of the steam room to give us time to finish whatever we were up to and take our places round her table for tea. We were her near-naked family while she poured from a big pot, not forgetting to put milk in mine, and passed around plates of ginger cake. She inquired pleasantly about wives, former loves, children, jobs. As far as I know, no one ever broke confidences. I loved her clean, soapy smell.

Though streetwise in a way I could not comprehend, she was so artless and innocent that I trusted her. I poured out to her all my experiences in the meeting house and church and told her that I had now decided to become a rabbi. She approved of the last, having had a hard time during the occupation herself. (She had a Jewish husband.)

But I did not come up to her standards in the sauna, though she never reproached me. One day she wanted me to meet another client, a gay, young Jewish man of good family, who was trying to put the pieces of his life together and tell his worried family. I panicked and told her never to tell him what I was. I avoided being alone with her afterwards. She understood and I understood myself and was not proud of it. That key Gospel line came to mind many times in the darkness and the steam: 'The truth shall make you free!'

I learnt a lot from her, in death as well as in life. Some years later, Tina got cancer and I visited her in hospital. On my next visit I was told she had died and the time and place of her funeral. Again, I panicked. I had come to give an ecumenical sermon in the city, and I was worried lest photographers turn up at the graveside to record all the *Mijnheers* who would certainly be there since she had done so much for them. I didn't dare risk it. 'And why should I?' I said to myself. She had helped so many, my absence wouldn't be noted in the crowd.

Later, I heard on the grapevine that few had come to her funeral – no reporters or photographers either. I felt sick with shame for not having honoured a good woman. I tried to blame religion, that had pushed me into such a situation. But this wouldn't wash. I was now my own religion – whatever was left of it was inside me and I could no longer duck responsibility. I had to accept my sin, being one of the mature men her sauna was for. Telling this story is my long-delayed tribute to her and replaces the lilies and roses I didn't bring.

But the rabbis said the real sign of repentance is not repeating your sin. 'The same woman, the same place', was the test of repentance, said one, though he could not know how I would apply his matter-of-fact advice. After some huffing and puffing, two steps forward and one step backward, many years later I came out and it was partly due to Tina. She made an honest rabbi of me!

Tina gave my religion a new direction, which would have surprised her. Through her I observed that the secular world was more spiritual than I expected, just as the religious world was more secular than I realised. More fundamental than ritual, theological systems, and the differences between denominations were straightforward goodness and generosity – whatever their clothing or lack of it. I wondered why this so startled me, because it had been said often enough in both Jewish and Christian Scriptures. It is so easy not to notice simplicity. The naked truth is the most difficult truth to see.

Christianity had shown me that God is seeking for us even more than we seek him. But like those involved in the encounter at Emmaus, we do not recognise what we bump into. In the steam, I became aware that God had crossed the North Sea with me, had accompanied me on the tram, and become conscious to me through his messenger Tina, his unknowing angel, just as he had met me long ago in my generous, medieval Jewish grand-mother, and had talked to me through the see-through friend in my imagination.

I had grown up! I no longer needed plastic angels with goldilocks and sweet smiles, because I had met the real thing in real life. I didn't have to go up to heaven, or search for truth in faraway places, as Moses said. I only had to see what was before my eyes and in my heart.

I never told Tina of the other spiritual experiences that awaited me in the darkness, behind the door she coaxed me through. I didn't expect such experiences at all in the cheerful, laddish, locker room stuff, the sexual rugger scrum laced with romance that I fell into. I watched cautiously and prudently the matings and partings, the manipulation and the generosity, the occasional recog-nition, as 'lovers' sometimes recognised a depth of feeling for each other.

Sexual desire is immediate and compulsive, and if

you're weak you're trodden down in the rush. But I met saintly people there too. I met the Frenchman who comforted and accommodated the older men, the coffin dodgers, for the sake of Jesus. I had never expected a meeting with an angel there.

I wasn't so theological or self-sacrificing. I was rather ruthless for I was angry at having been suppressed for so long. I was also discontented and disoriented. Where was the way for me in all this? 'Help!' I cried to no one in particular, repeating my invocation made at the Quaker meeting. Once again, I had invoked my old see-through mate. In my imagination he sat in the steam, wearing a towel that wouldn't quite meet like mine. Which was suitable as I now knew he was inner not outer – he was in me.

Sitting naked in that naked place, I could speak to him about the naked truth. I disentangled my limbs and let the questions form in me. 'Why do I get so little out of all this?' I wondered discontentedly. 'Is a few seconds' release all there is to it? Is this what I've been mooning over in committee rooms, tutorials and libraries? Is sex a cheat too?' I closed my eyes and nearly wept in anger and self-pity.

'You don't get much, Lionel,' said my inner voice, 'because you don't give much. You've got to risk more, be more generous, more open! Allow yourself to meet real people, not fantasies. Risk it. If a little love should happen, don't run away like a scalded cat!'

My prayer had again turned inside out. It had become a boomerang, which winged its way back to me. I had thought of life as a problem for so long that I had forgotten the joy of life. I didn't know how to recognise happiness or how to cope with it when it was in front of me.

'What do I do? How do I behave?' I asked urgently.

'Well,' said my see-through friend judiciously, 'you could start by keeping appointments, even if you've met someone more attractive in the meantime. And if you do say "no", you could say "no" nicely, especially if you're saying "no" to an oldie. Be polite, like your French friend over there.'

Slowly, all the angels, messengers and voices of this world and the world beyond melted together and spoke through my inner voice, teaching me the ten commandments of sauna life. They were the moon, my guardian angel; Jesus, my inner voice; my Granny; my Emmaus discoveries; the self-sacrificing comrades who had given their lives; all the goodness I had ever stumbled across in life. They coalesced into my inner rabbi, my teacher who followed me inside and outside organisations, without prejudice.

After that, we went everywhere together and my life in Amsterdam turned inside out. That voice whispered in my ear in dance halls and clubs. I seemed to see my friend's presence a few tables up. And when a climax was over, my voice, my partner and I made a threesome because he – the spirit now – was the affection between us – this affection stopped me withdrawing and running away as if I were ashamed after I had satisfied myself. I now tried to listen to the needs of another person and satisfy him.

In the early hours of the morning, when all places of worship were locked, the twinkling bottles on the bars became the eternal lights on his arks and altars. Psychosis? Schizophrenia? I can only say the proof of the pudding is in the eating, and what I saw and heard led me back into decency (the real sort, not the respectable imitation), laughter and life – I got them more abundantly.

I was so much easier with him now that I didn't have to speak to him in jargon, minding dogmatic p's and q's, and putting on po-faced, pious looks. When a couple see each other wearing towels that don't meet around their middles, they know each other as intimately as meditation.

I wasn't afraid of being honest with him either.

'Can I ask you something?' I said. 'Do you mind me not being a Christian? It just doesn't feel right. It doesn't feel like home.'

'I don't mind what you call yourself or me,' he said, uninterestedly. 'I never called myself a Christian. I'm there for you, if you want me and use me, that's all. I enjoy you. You make me laugh.'

'Would you mind, then,' I said after some thought, 'if you became my rabbi, inner voice or guardian angel?'

'You're in charge,' he answered, 'but don't waste time on what doesn't matter. Why give yourself so many problems, Lionel, which are not yours? Just enjoy yourself without hurting anybody! That's difficult enough!' he added, and sighed.

I giggled nervously because at last I was beginning to cut loose from a dead past, make peace with myself and like myself. The naked truth had set me free. But I couldn't use my freedom because I didn't know how you came to heaven through happiness. Happiness finally broke through to me in a way I had never expected. I found it through sailing. I had no sense of balance and little sense of direction, but I could cook and pray in a gale and even overcome the epilepsy (grand mal) which was beginning to show itself. The luminous beauty of it all and the aloneness of our boat brought back my moon, my angel and my friend.

This was far from the grim vigil in that church in

England, and it posed problems I hadn't expected.

'I'm your friend, mate,' he interrupted. 'I'm no more Christian than you are. Don't turn me into another ecclesiastical problem.' I've tried not to, ever since, but if you're professionally religious it isn't easy breaking loose from labels and copyright and such. I was so pleased he hadn't disappeared on me and we'd journey together like I used to with the moon. I tried to see him at that time in all the partners I slept with. The affection that ensued made up for my lack of experience. Sex on its own could be grim and addictive. The divine mystery brought back the magic.

17

Muddling My Way to Marriage

'You must sit down,' says Love, 'and taste my meat.'
So I did sit and eat.

George Herbert (1593–1633)

If you find some special delicacy that will keep,
reserve it to honour the Sabbath.

Kitzur Shulchan Aruch – a popular
summary of Jewish law and practice.

You can't spend your life in a sauna, fascinating though it
was with its insights into heaven and hell. Sooner or later
you have to come up for air. I did, and decided on a Jewish
marriage. I thought it would be simple. I'd meet Mr Right
and we would be faithful and happy for the rest of our
lives. In the event, I tried three times and it was a case of
third time lucky. I had so much to learn. Only when I was
fifty did the message get home, and I dealt with the reality
of my partner not my fantasy of him, and my love for a
person not an institution. Still, better late than never.
Some people never get that far, hetero or homo.

A gay marriage or commitment ceremony – I am not
interested in labels but lives – is more difficult than a
hetero one. It's a more complicated fit, socially, psycho-
logically and physically though the ends are the same:

commitment, trust and leading each other into happiness. Socially it was and still is very difficult, and before such relationships were decriminalised in Britain in 1968, almost impossible. Judaism, which welds hetero marriages together, used to destroy gay ones and sometimes still does.

Jewish 'friends' used to feel a pious zeal in breaking up what had taken so much sacrifice to put together. Clerical colleagues and their wives vied with each other in inviting me but never my partner and placing me next to unattached females. My partner and I had to pretend we were each other's lodgers; we had to invent mythical girlfriends; lie, lie, lie and fib, fib, fib. I was at a Jewish conference when my partner was ill. He couldn't stay with me at the same hotel but was in the one next door, where secretly and furtively I used to visit him and see to his needs. At such times, I sighed for the clean, straightforward honesty of my Dutch sauna. I wanted to return to Amsterdam, not for orgies but for honesty. Jesus had his criticisms of the establishment and so had I. I felt for him.

Since I never expected any help or understanding from Judaism or Christianity, I didn't feel hurt when I didn't get any. The only ones who counselled me were my therapist and my inner voice. Christianity was too preoccupied with virgins and Judaism with procreation and respectability to be helpful. I went for advice to a rabbi and got thrown out; and to a priest who shillied and shallied so much that I took pity on the tormented man and dropped the subject. His Christianity had tangled him up even more than me.

When formal religion doesn't work, you have to go to God direct. He led me to the faithful, committed relationship I now very much enjoy and my partner and I thank him by lighting candles on Friday night as my grand-mother did. For outsiders like me, spirituality isn't a luxury but what we live on, our daily bread.

That's why I'm grateful to Christianity for showing me that there was a private hot line to the divine, provided you were self-critical and didn't confuse conscience with schizophrenia. I'm also grateful to Christianity for teaching me a lot about love. My best teachers, curiously enough, were the religious celibates I got to know – nuns, monks and friars. The nuns were the most matter-of-fact and the least scared. I learnt from them that sex was one way into loving but there were other ways too, if you had enough belief and were built that way, with more powers of sublimation than me. It was a chancy affair. Some religious managed to divert their sexual energy into spiritual energy and became contemplatives, and some, who misjudged their capacities, ended up as alcoholics, depressives or tranquilliser addicts. Their Christian enthusiasm did not help them to be realistic about their own make-up.

The nuns, monks and friars introduced me to the Christian mystics. I learnt a lot about passion from them, because they are the world's great lovers, though you have to weed out the kinky, sadomasochistic bits. I certainly began to comprehend the difference between the heights and depths they described and my own shallow, passing romances. They showed me something deeper that I hadn't experienced, but I believed it existed because they said so. Their writings and their lives convinced me of it. They were sometimes hysterical but still shrewd cookies. Meditating on them led me out of the numbers game into depth, and concern with quality, not quantity. I knew I'd absorbed a lot because that's when I began to understand the price you pay for real relationships, the giving up you can't avoid. Giving up! It was odd how something so small and domestic connected up with the saints I'd read about in Bede.

In the late fifties those mystics, Christian and Jewish (for I'd discovered the early Jewish Chassidim by then) showed me how to recognise the divine spark, God's image, in others. For a brief moment, my partner became 'holy unto me' as in the Jewish marriage service.

This was an advance. Another help from Christianity was its outreach, by which I do not mean pushy evangelism but seeing the divine in unfamiliar places. I met a lot of loving people who were Christian, who were beyond the pluses and minuses of their egos and beyond respectability too. The Christian establishment didn't relate much – it was too judgmental about what it didn't know. But individual Christians, who sailed into unknown theological territory, relying on God within them as their compass, as the early Celtic saints did, meant a lot.

Judaism then began to come closer to me, after the excitement and romance of sex simmered down and I needed to learn how to continue a relationship, not initiate or end one. I tentatively began to integrate bits of Judaism into my own circumstances, pragmatically and experimentally. Many traditional ceremonies and cycles still worked, provided I didn't use them to play holy families or for show or uniformity. They helped me make a home out of a love-nest. I hallowed our Friday night meal, using my grandmother's recipes for food and faith. The *petit soins* of Judaism, the homely *mitzvot* (the practices of a rabbinic lifestyle) fell into place and reconnected with my childhood and the awareness of holiness which had preceded my Christian experience.

How much of my Jewish past could I rebuild? The great extended family of my childhood had eroded away. Yet tucked away in the Jewish past were the *chavurot* – the holy friendship circles of former times – rather like house churches. Jesus and his disciples were probably one of them. They united gays like me and other outsiders into a new sort of family based on ties of friendship, not blood. I was astonished how Judaism could create community, making homes out of houses and creating villages and hamlets in faceless suburbs. I was impressed by its power to stick couples together with its own holy glue. I had, of course, preached about that glue in marriage sermons but now I could give it my personal recommendation.

As regards physical love, neither Judaism nor Christianity was helpful. I had to learn elsewhere how to make up in bed after a row – the sensitivity, imagination and give-and-take that good loving requires. I thank my partners who had to put up with my first clumsy and crude attempts at love and who coped with my panics. I thank, too, the honest hippies I met in Amsterdam.

Gradually all the bits began to fall into place, the pious bits and the body bits – and I learnt in middle age what I ought to have known in my teens. I find it hard to forgive religion for the ignorance it inflicted on me when I was young.

One day, when I was more than usually morose, my assistant said to me, 'You've got to find a friend, Lionel.'

'I don't know how,' I replied. 'I'm too old for gay bars and discos and that sort of thing.'

'Well, what about those papers you sometimes read?' said my assistant.

'They're all about partners fifty years old, who look forty-nine in the dark and are into leather underwear. That's not for me.' But I did look through the gay paper again and I spotted this unadorned advert:

Merseyside – ordinary, working-class guy, fifties, seeks partner, age and looks unimportant.

To show willing, I dashed off a short reply and was astonished when Merseyside telephoned me three weeks later. It took us three years before we came back from a holiday still speaking, and we didn't and don't share the same political, cultural or gastronomic tastes. We never buy the same newspapers. But we've been together now for nearly twenty years, faithful, committed and caring, with occasional blow-ups, usually settled by humour, prayers, kisses and cuddles. We've worked out our own religious patterns without benefit of clergy. I'm grateful in part, but only in part, to Judaism and Christianity. They had become very selfish, middle-class preserves with no liking for minorities. Their morality had dwindled to 'Blow you, Jack, I'm all right', but they contributed some essential pieces of life's jigsaw. So I'll be generous – one and a half cheers to both of them!

18

Divorce and Death

Christianity is good at loss, and more relevant for failure than success because it turns loss and failure inside out. So though it didn't teach me much about marriage, paradoxically it gave me a lesson in divorce – how to turn the love and passion of past times into continuing affection and friendship. This came about through another meeting with the friend in my imagination.

An important relationship ended in Venice. I knew it even if my earthly friend didn't. I took refuge in a Venetian church to get some inner quiet and because I felt sore, more with myself than with him, and with life because it had carried us away from each other. In the dusty murk, this message which I think about a lot formed itself within me.

'Don't get so steamed up. This wasn't your first break-up and it won't be your last. You'll survive. In this life, you taste love only in your prayers and relationships. But one day (I assumed this was when I was dying) you'll meet the real thing.' These unexpected thoughts lightened my load, and my partner and I managed to dine decently with each other, despite all that we couldn't say.

The consequences of our ungay 'divorce' turned out as expected – the same hurt feelings, the same rows about who owned this pot or that doorknocker. They are the common coin of hurt. Breaking up a home of many years is traumatic. We were just about to have a corker of yet another row, when I suddenly seemed to sense my old mate winking at me through my friend's face. It was so comic that I giggled.

'Let's play double or quits for it in the pub,' I said.

'That's the most sensible thing you've said for years, Lionel,' my partner replied.

We did, and we still see each other regularly. Both of us have acquired new partners, but the affection between us endures and grows steadily and we know we have learnt a lot from each other, from which our present partners benefit and for which we thank whoever, whatever. You need a lot of real religion for a divorce. More love is required than for marriage. Perhaps that's why it isn't so odd that Christianity was so helpful.

Later on, when we had untied ourselves peaceably enough, my mind returned to that conversation in the church. It had touched on my divorce from this life too, though I hadn't registered it at the time, and that was more important than divorce from any friend. It changed my attitude to the old age I would soon enter because it changed my attitude to dying.

Old age is not what it was in my grandparents' time. There is a lot to be said for it. Some of it is very nice, like my state pension and bus pass. On a less material level, you are free from expectation, especially if you've been prudent and added to that pension. What you have done, you've done and the rest is gravy. There is no rotting away by the fire. You trade in the holiday brochures featuring bikinis and bosoms (though on reflection, many don't do that either), for winter brochures with pictures of oldies singing merrily and keeping fit with aerobics and line dancing, whiling away the winters, making friends at

bingo and enemies at bridge. It is better than bearable if
you have worked out your ideas about how you will deal
with your own death. That comes not just from me but
from the master himself – Sigmund Freud. He said that
you cannot know how to live until you know how to die.

The death horizon comes steadily closer, and the
spiritual lesson we have to learn is not an easy one. Here,
pragmatic Judaism helped me. The rabbis did not think
this world was meant for happiness or unhappiness. It
was a school where you had to learn two lessons before
you moved on, which were how to acquire things and
how to give them up as gracefully as you were able. The
first is the normal lesson for youth; the second for old
age. Sooner or later in that latter part of life, you realise
how it all has to be given back, your possessions, your
memory, your loved ones and your life. If this giving up
has a meaning for you, it becomes easier and more
interesting. Reading Bede at Oxford had interested me in
the lesson of giving up. Mortality also gives you pause in
a competitive society. It may make you nicer, though not
always.

Death is so personal that we all have to work it out for
ourselves. A friend of mine recently decided to die in his
own time and in his own place. His family had looked
after him lovingly during his terminal illness. But now
the medicos said he must go into hospital for the final
paralysis. He was not burdened by religious dogmas, and
after consulting his family and friends, checking the
formalities through with his doctors and arranging his
affairs and his funeral, he gave a quiet, pleasant party to
make his farewells. During the party he asked a friend
to pass him a draught, and exited without fuss. In his
country, this was permitted.

He was a considerate man and he had every right to

pass away as he wished. I'd like the right, if I can think clearly, to control my own medication against pain. I'm not good at pain and I don't see why someone else should control something so personal to me. I don't want to be bossed or bullied by other people's religion or ideologies.

But for myself, I'd prefer to let my own death take its course because my view of life is different from that of my dying friend, partly because of my experience in Venice.

I'm curious about dying. It might be the greatest adventure of my life. It might be my new birth seen from the other end. With all that morphine, it's bound to be a giggle!

Death itself doesn't worry me – I think – provided the pain is controlled, of course. Like most Jews, I'm not tormented by a sadist's hell or a nit-picking judgment. I've actually been near death twice in my life and at both times I felt relief. Before I went into hospital for what I thought was the last time, I treated myself to a double portion of curry and then stuffed a Bible for respectability and *Gentlemen Prefer Blondes* for enjoyment into my night bag. I'd done this world just as I'd done my job in my little ecclesiastical court, and was now interested in what came next.

I did shiver a bit because what came next seemed like a black hole. But then I remembered all the other black holes in my life, my problems which I'd cursed at the time. But at Oxford my problems had turned inside out. I had grown through them. Without them I don't think I'd ever have become a rabbi, but a suburban property solicitor or a wino. And a strange enlightenment had come from my relationship problems, too. So from those experiences I trusted that there would be a light in this final black hole. That's not exactly faith, which I've never been good at, but trust, which is more reasonable.

But now I had to add on that experience in the church in Venice. It certainly helped me with divorce, as I've said. But it also seemed to refer to death too. In which case, dying may also turn inside out. I won't go in the dignified, arranged way my friend chose. Unlike him, I am a believer in my own idiosyncratic way, and in dying I have an appointment I mustn't miss.

I had a sense that the different ingredients of my life and faith were cooking together. The agony was unnecessary. The problem belonged to other people, not me. My mate would see me through.

19

Brother Blue

In the first degree of contemplation the soul is led
into itself and gathered within itself. In the second
degree man sees what he is so gathered together. In
the third degree man lifts himself above himself and
takes pains to look upon God within himself.

St Edmund of Abingdon (1175–1240)
quoted in *The English Spirit*, DLT

In this life, we experience occasional anticipations
of heaven. We also experience occasional anticipations of death and resurrection. The rabbis called waking
up in the morning the little resurrection, for sleep was an
anticipation of death. My dog experienced my death every
time I walked out of the front door without her, and
resurrection when I miraculously re-entered the world
of her senses. I used to experience a kind of death
whenever I visited a contemplative friary or monastery,
which is why part of me manufactured so many excuses
to avoid the journey. The Catholic smells were different
from the spicy Jewish smells I was used to. The images
disturbed me, and I was worried lest I should ever feel a
call to such a place.

Though I never became a monk (nor a card-carrying
Christian), I still felt called to monasteries, friaries and

nunneries, and miss them in my own Judaism. Ordinary services are too long, and too crowded to experience God – apart from those on the Day of Atonement. So much has to be said that there is no time to listen. And in England, most services are either formal and deadly, or clappy-happy. They function in the main for communal solidarity, not for personal enlightenment. For me, they serve as an introduction to the inner prayer and contemplation which come later.

But I need to renew my toehold in heaven and my need is urgent. Despite all their monastic, medieval longings which I don't share, some monasteries and friaries are meant for just that. I don't mind a bit of unobtrusive company too, because we are all on the same wavelength. I have tried to translate something of their spirit into my Jewish world by encouraging retreats. I am pleased to act as an ecumenical go-between without the usual propaganda or zealotry. Quietness and privacy are necessary if you have fallen in love with God, or if you have just fallen in love.

Such an acquaintance develops its own logic – favourite places to meet, times for chatter and for silence, odd presents and odd demands at unexpected times. What Christianity gave me was neither a practice nor a dogma, neither a set of doctrines nor a liturgy, but an intimacy with an inner voice, a friend. This was a new way of regarding religion, or a very old way if I connected it with my childhood imaginations. My Christianity had started off as an affair powered by unhappiness and sublimation with a messenger, an angel or the Jesus I bumped into in the silence.

Later, the romantic elements dropped away, as I tasted normal, earthly, humdrum happiness. At first I was in panic. I didn't think I could go it alone. I was dependent on the romance. Besides the spiritual pluses, it gave me status, a second-best love in case the earthly type went wrong, a kind of celestial insurance, and an 'in' with the cosmos. But I calmed down. I had outgrown the frou-frou of faith. Now I often had only an inner voice and that supportive silence. But that same something, some-one, was still at work within it whether I used imaginative devices or not. I recognised it. Also, when I recognised that something in others, or invoked it plain or per-sonalised, the same deep well of love and generosity surged up inside me, attesting its presence.

My various therapists and my own reasoning wonder if this is all inside me. Voices and such make them uneasy, and I don't blame them because they worry me as well. Some may have suspected schizoid tendencies or child-hood dependence, and they may have been right. I don't know enough about neuroses or psychoses to gainsay them. But in my imagination and experience, this contact doesn't feel as if it were only inside me. It also feels as if something or someone is trying to reach out towards me, just as I am trying to reach out towards it or him or her. Though you neither see it nor hear it, you experience it or him or her.

I don't experience him much in crowds of any kind of any denomination. I experience him much more in silent, fairly empty places of worship. I became conscious of a presence at Friday evening services in winter, when my only congregation were the chairman and organist of my synagogue. I experience him now at monasteries and friaries of the humbler sort. They have been the Christian gift to me. With all their oddities, they open the way into the kingdom of heaven inside or outside me. Sometimes the experience is frightening. Usually it is a coming home.

For some years I have been drawn to a Carmelite priory

near Oxford, though I don't feel I have to haunt the place. My voice seems to want it. But then, why do friends want to meet at some particular café? Why do lovers tryst at the same park bench? It's that sort of situation.

My intellect tells me that God is everywhere, and so are his messengers, so really it isn't necessary to drag a suitcase to Paddington, especially as I live on London's inconvenient Northern Line. I could drop into the chapel of the college where I teach, I tell myself.

But that won't work. I know it. Though the chapel is a gentle place, it's usually occupied by purposeful groups, doing good and discussing therapy or scholarship, and I feel guilty at wanting a whole room for private meditation – an uneconomic luxury. That is why priories and monasteries are needed. They recognise the primacy of that inner conversation and don't think you're nuts, dragging your suitcase to the wilds of suburban Oxford. Whatever our different dogmas, and dogmatically there is a chasm between the friars and me, I think we share an experience.

There are other less exalted reasons for my visit. The fathers and brothers like me, the food is of the comforting nursery kind, I get no letters or telephone calls other than those of my own choosing and, having little sense of order, I feel better when semi-institutionalised, with life regulated by bells. When I get there, I munch a biscuit or two or three as comfort food against the culture shock and sidle into the chapel, unworried if I'm not alone because whoever's there will be on the same wavelength and I say hello to heaven.

Heaven has its own magic, and it turns my low into a high. I know now my journey was worthwhile because I am no longer straining after religion. I just let whatever happens, happen. This is a relief because it releases me from the rat race and worldly success and failure, and other-worldly success and failure too. It is easy to be enslaved by them if you are a public figure like a minister. You just join the role-playing which goes along with the job. My world then starts to turn inside out as it did in 1950. I start to feel gloriously happy. It's fun finding it, him or her again. I've come to the right address.

I waste my time with silly speculations. Should I have become a monk or friar? Poverty I could cope with. The worry of it was part of my childhood and after that, the stylised poverty of monastic life would seem a doddle. But obedience was not part of my anarchist nature. Whom should I be obedient to? I don't trust any organisations because I've directed too many. Chastity would be even weirder in such an all-male setting. It might not guard me but inflame me. Also I was shrewd enough to spot the difference between being a visitor to a monastery or friary and being a signed-up member. On closer inspection, communal life might not be a foretaste of the company of heaven or a large jolly, Jewish, extended family but more like a penance such as some dreadful cruise ship where you can't avoid your fellow-passengers. I decided that you really needed to have a lot of Christian belief to become a Christian monk or friar. The obviousness and banality of this only struck me comparatively recently. And such belief I don't have, though I have been near it. Also, liturgy and ritual were never that important for me, and I realise that the Eucharist was for them beyond any ritual or liturgy but I was outside it.

But in the silence I also realise that not only was my journey worthwhile but so were its inner questionings, difficulties and struggles. The latter are essential (another inside out). Otherwise you're just a Jewish junkie and spiritual hedonist on another trip. You have to show you mean business. My token sacrifices (London's crumbling Northern Line), and doubts at least convince me that I'm serious. At home I'm too surrounded by my mementoes, bits and books for anything to happen. Nothing from another dimension can get to me. I'm too protected. I understand why the prophets went out into the desert, Jesus into the wilderness, the Baal Shem into the Carpathian Mountains. My priory is too chintzy and cosy to be a desert. But it's a stand-in for one, because of that sense of desolation and displacement which comes when I wander too far from my Jewish roots.

In the empty chapel, I try to get a foretaste of what's going to happen or what I'll make happen during my brief stay. My prayer life has changed a lot since those first, fine raptures when I was a student at Oxford. Then I had the same moony look on my face as I notice on new devotees now. But it was what I needed at the time, and I went through a lot of hoops trying to make the romance real, which it partly, but only partly, became. And yet, sometimes with all my reservations, I know I glimpsed nuggets of truth which startled me, which were not just inside out but way out. I even leapt over the culture shock and made lasting contact with Teresa, John and Thérèse, though I can't see their relevance to the sufferings of the Holocaust.

Most of that's changed now. After I've said hello, I relax and let the silence cleanse me like a ritual bath. Heaven will eventually show its hand. I'm prepared to use artificial aids now as a stimulant, just as couples in love have their own turn-ons. I take a book with me and tranquilly dip into the predigested thoughts of someone else. I read a bit, stop, and the book acts as a diving-board into the silence. I do the same with some Arab worry beads, turning them into an unofficial rosary or

Jewish prayer straps. Then I start off by thinking about what I normally think about, such as whether we'll have fried onions for supper, and where should I go on holiday after I've scampered back to Golders Green, smoked salmon and civilisation.

The start doesn't matter. In a place of prayer, you only need to let God in. And he will draw the threads to himself. In no time, my onions sizzle mystically.

When the fathers, brothers and retreatants are saying their office, I no longer agonise, as I used to, about what I should or shouldn't say. That's God's business, not mine. I am moved when they take communion, but the same God comes to me differently. I also keep quiet when they recite, 'O God, you're wonderful, marvellous, all-wise, all-loving, the tops . . .' I can't recite such prayers for two reasons. One is the Holocaust, as I've said before. Another is a remark my mother made after watching some female mother octopus or squid eating her male partner on TV.

'Oh, Lionel,' she said, 'couldn't it have been organised better?' I agree with her, so I have had to work out what God I worship, which isn't easy, and a label won't do.

At present I worship the God in us, and outside us, who redeems tragedy, who brings good out of evil and meaning out of madness. I have experienced him. Fingering the Arab prayer beads in my pocket, I think of that power living in Anne Frank, Franz Jäggerstätter, my grandmother, my mother and father, Janusz Korczak, in Jesus, in those people in the camps who comforted newcomers with their last bit of bread, and in me.

That's enough for my first 'conversation' in the chapel. Those conversations always make me hungry, and soon it's time for thick bread, marge and marmalade.

In another conversation, I try to separate my faith from magic. And in another, my self begins to move a

centimetre away from my own centre towards hers, his
or heaven's, and I feel a moment of glory which I can't
sustain. This moves me to buy pious books that I shall
never read, and my face composes itself into that constipated expression which shows I'm on a high that I can't
handle. But my impish inner voice says, 'Attaboy, Lionel,
I'll go and grow with you.' I realise then that it's time to
depart. When no one's looking I say goodbye and blow a
kiss towards the sanctuary light. I know it's not what
rabbis are supposed to do, but I can't say nothing. That's
not how friends and affurs behave. So, '*Adieu, mon cher
ami, adieu!*'

20

Bottom-side-up at the BEEB

All the bits of my religion didn't only fuse in the inner voice I heard on retreats but also in my own disembodied voice over the radio. It was the listeners, their unobtrusive spirituality and their needs which helped to fuse them. I didn't just give spirituality to those people – they gave it to me. They gave me a vocation which required everything I had, whatever its provenance.

I got on to the radio at the end of the fifties. I was first asked to give little sermonettes, 'God-slots', for commercial radio, and then prayers or 'thoughts' on the BBC, mostly in the early morning before breakfast. It came about by chance. I never expected to continue over the years. I didn't think I had enough thoughts in me. Also, I didn't know at the beginning how deeply they would affect me. I've continued giving them ever since and they taught me to see religion not just inside out but also bottom-side-up, not from the theological heights, but from the needs of ordinary folk wherever they were in life. It was ordinary life which brought everything together – my Christian experiences, my Jewish home and many other bits too – anything which was genuine, generous and hopeful. You can bluff these qualities high up on a pulpit but not before a mike.

A studio was not like a synagogue, as I quickly

discovered. For one thing, I could not quote traditional Scriptures because my radio congregation was multi-faith or no faith at all. It was no use repeating the customary formulas, 'the sages say . . .' or 'it is written in the prophets'. They neither knew those prophets and sages nor recognised their credentials. That applied to Moses, Jesus and all the spiritual mega-stars. It was a level playing field of disbelief.

A rabbi I knew deplored the absence of a great religious visionary for our time, one who could point the way ahead for doubters. He pointed to past crises in Jewish history, each marked tidily with its own visionary and a new book. (The book of the Second World War was not written by a rabbi, but by an adolescent girl, Anne Frank.)

But I don't think any spiritual mega-star will come to us now because in a democratic age, God speaks democratically. Bits of our personal stories will gradually coalesce into unofficial scriptures which will point a variety of holy ways ahead. If there are enough of such stories, they will cancel out each other's quirkiness.

I did notice the urgent, though covered, spiritual quest in my radio congregation. I could sense it. It came out of their need to survive without losing their integrity in a competitive world. My listeners weren't saints, but neither was I. They learnt from me. I learnt from them. It was a two-way communication. And my contribution included a Quaker bit, a monastic bit and a Jewish bit, among many other bits.

The religious situation was like 'pick and mix' therapy or counselling. A long time ago at the birth of analysis, they were all worried about names and labels. You were a Jungian, a Freudian, a Kleinian, a Reichian. But separating them in real life didn't make sense. Different clients with different needs and temperaments required different approaches at different times, and most therapists now use all of them for the benefit of their clients. Religions are still too uptight to be as open as this. It is still a case of 'me Jew, you Christian', though after the last war, we are all faced with the same problems and are giving more or less the same answers.

I learnt a lot from analysis and therapy, including one lesson that went to the heart of modern religious problems. That lesson was especially suitable for an ecumenical radio congregation with all the shades of belief, half-belief and unbelief you can think of. It wasn't my job to do PR for my own lot in my few minutes of broadcasting time, nor was it my job to plaster my own religious solutions on my listeners. It was my job to help them identify and interpret their own religious experience and experience of life so that they could work out their own answers to their own lives. Sometimes I could help them by showing how I was tackling my own problems. This required a depth of honesty which is unusual in a pulpit.

This was very different from the advice of my elders and betters when I first started this radio work. Some colleagues told me to instruct my new congregation in the Jewish problem, or give lessons in easy Talmud. But my common sense and inner voice both rejected PR, however pious.

'It's not what you want to say, but what helps your listeners' needs,' said my inner voice firmly. 'It's not fair, when they've got so many problems, to serve them the Jewish problem with their cornflakes.'

So under this guidance I started to meditate about the needs of my new radio congregation instead, however ordinary they were. They needed courage to get out of bed on a rainy Monday morning in a recession and not dive back under their duvet. They needed to keep their self-esteem at the job centre, survive the desolation when their partner walked out on them or vice versa. They needed strength not to be enslaved by the rat race or by the false gods of success, and to keep their temper while swearing blue murder in a traffic jam. To answer these needs, I had to draw on my experiences from anywhere and everywhere – from synagogues, churches and saunas, Quaker silences and Sabbath candles, from Teresa, Thérèse, Franz Jaegerstaedter, Chassidic rabbis, Yiddish jokes, Marx, Jesus, Moses and anybody who was a genuine spiritual somebody or nobody. I couldn't afford to be choosy or bother about labels because the needs were immediate and I was only allowed a few minutes to try to deal with them.

Having had a Christian experience myself was a great help because most of my listeners were nominally Christian. Therefore I could understand the love Jesus might have inspired in them once, and which still lingered in their lives. That Christian love had also pierced me, for no spiritual affair was exclusive for me, only the physical one, as I had told the baffled young man at the party. Before the green light flashed in the studio and I was on the air, I remembered my own religious re-awakening in November 1950.

This made me feel very close to the people at the other end of the mike. It rescued me from disputation points. I just shared with them anything I knew in Judaism which could help. I hadn't realised till then how Jewish Jesus was, though more apocalyptic than I was used to or liked.

I was surprised how well all my bits fitted together over the radio. And this helped me put my own life together. What helped the listeners also healed my own inner fissures and divisions. The wisdom was the same, whatever the label. The problem was the frame, not the content.

But that's enough about my congregation's needs. What I needed most was love for listeners I could never see or meet. So before the green light winked and I was on, I invoked Jesus in my Christian listeners, the goodness in my agnostic ones and whoever helped me get into my heaven mode – often the friend I met at that Quaker meeting. When I did this, my voice softened, and a surge of affection rose within me, illuminating them and me together. That is the best way of describing it.

All the bits of our experience which in theory cannot fit together nice and tidily in this world, can work together in practice. I learnt that what we cannot comprehend intellectually, we can still use for good. This is how the Christian experience melted into my Jewish devotions and lifestyle.

Two sayings helped me. The first came from my former analyst who, on his return from India where he had slept on the pavements of Bombay and found enlightenment in an ashram in the foothills of the Himalayas, had been asked by curious friends, 'Did you meet a great guru?' He had answered in the affirmative because the greatest guru is life. Life and its demands help more than apologetics. In Vedantic terms, I was both karma yoga and bhakti yoga. They were my Judaism and Christian experience. Ordinary life was integrating them for me.

The second saying came from my teacher, Leo Baeck, the Chief Rabbi of Germany in the Nazi time, who had survived concentration camp.

'Judaism,' he said, 'is your religious home, Lionel. It is not your religious prison.'

What helped me just as much or more than these

sayings were my listeners, who saved me because they weren't into role-playing. In matters of religion they didn't put on the style. They didn't know how. They were genuinely humble. They didn't claim to know the lot like a lot of religious establishments.

Later on, when I assisted at alcoholic or HIV retreats, the same thing happened. What was impossible in theology became necessary in practice. Life, the great guru, was answering my problems. Some people venerate a saint, a tsaddik (a sort of Jewish saint), or some spiritual writer. I venerate them too – up to a point. But my greatest teacher has been life, which skilfully and quietly fits the pieces of my inner jigsaw gently together, as it does yours if you let it.

As the traditional Jewish toast says, '*L'Hayyim*!' – 'To Life!'

21

Meditating before a God

> In every age I came back
> to deliver the holy,
> to destroy the sin of the sinner,
> to establish righteousness . . .
> Whatever path men travel
> Is my path:
> No matter where they walk
> It leads to me.
>
> The Song of God, from *Bhagavad-Gita*,
> trans. by Swami Prabhavananda and
> Christopher Isherwood.

Trying to slot so many experiences into a staid rabbinical training wasn't easy. I felt trapped in an ecclesiastical cul-de-sac or like a laboratory mouse running round in talmudic circles. All attempts to sort it out theologically came to an abrupt halt because I bore the marks of too many faiths and ideologies. A Christian friend said he could sort me out on classical Evangelical lines.

'OK,' I said amiably. 'Try!'

'Well,' he said. 'You believe in the Messiah, of course.'

I scratched my head and replied, 'I don't really.'

He looked startled and I explained that I had followed too many messiahs and I no longer expected any of them to drop from the skies to sort out my problems – that was the illusion of children. I needed to find my redeemer in me, become a mini-redeemer as far as I could, for myself and others.

'Well, what do you believe in?' he said.

It was a fair question and I tried to answer it honestly.

'I know there's a power of redemption that works through all of us if we allow it to use us, which brings good out of evil, niceness out of nastiness, bliss out of tragedy, and that for some it can wear a human face. I've experienced it.'

We shelved my conversion after that, which was only sensible. After all, there have been so many Jewish-Christian disputations and, as my late colleague Rabbi Hugo Gryn used to say, 'Whichever way you slice the salami, Lionel, it's still the same salami.'

But I did discover another way which illuminated the Jewish-Christian divide in a more revealing light. I stumbled across it because my former Reichian analyst ended up as a Vedantist, making it to an Indian ashram way ahead of the Beatles and the flower-power people. I was intrigued because that's where Christopher Isherwood ended up too, though his ashram was in California not India, and he didn't have to renounce his gayness or hide himself in a closet or pretend his lovers had never happened. I read his translation of the *Gita* and a romantic novel about a young Westerner becoming a Hindu monk. Of course I promptly had ideas of doing the same, but I decided my poor mother had had enough for a while. Later, I found I wasn't the only young Jew on this track and in America it was already the subject of Jewish jokes – like this.

A woman wanders through India, head cast down, searching for the holiest guru of all, till finally they tell her the wisest teacher lives high up on a peak of the Himalayas, and only sherpas can get her to him.

'Bring me sherpas!' she says, and with them makes her way to a solitary monastery in a blizzard.

'Take me to your teacher!' she tells the gatekeeper.

'It would be no use,' he replies, 'his eyes are turned inwards in profoundest contemplation.'

She begs again and the despairing gatekeeper takes her into his presence. The guru's eyes are sunk in the profoundest contemplation as she had been told. The woman looks up and then exclaims in a firm Bronx voice, 'Alvin, this time you've gone too far – and you need a clean loincloth!'

That was my situation. If my parents were going to commit suicide over my becoming a Christian monk, what would they do if I turned up in Golders Green as a Hindu monk with a shorn head, orange robes and a begging bowl? I remembered a distant cousin who had announced her forthcoming marriage to a gentle Burmese student.

'Ach,' said my great aunt piteously, 'he's not even a *goy* (Jewish for Gentile)!'

Fortunately for my family I never got nearer to India than a house in Muswell Hill, where in clean underwear I meditated in front of a god before breakfast. I never really felt comfortable with idol- or image-worship, whatever form it took, though I could get used to it. In synagogues the Torah scrolls had been turned into semi-idols. People kissed and cuddled them as they were borne around in procession. For me, books are meant to be read, not cuddled. And it felt the same with the Eucharist in Christianity. Bread should be eaten, not adored. It was the Marxist, Puritan part of me which made me narrow-minded.

Sitting cross-legged in front of the god – which was not easy because Jews are not built that way, their behinds are too big – my mind wandered to the babushka which a Marxist friend had brought me back from the Soviet-Union-that-was. It was one of those Russian dolls that open up to reveal another and yet another inside it. I also meditated on the game of bridge which I was just learning. The two-dimensional reality of playing cards was enclosed in the more comprehensive three-dimensional world of consumer objects, which was itself enclosed in the more comprehensive world of the spirit and that itself was enclosed in realities beyond my understanding. A cosmic babushka!

In the same way, within the angels, the spirits, the prophet Elijah, the moon, my half-historical, half-mythical Jesus and God with his male sex and human passions – all of which enter our lives through our imagination, either because we summon them out of need or they summon us out of love – Judaism knows a Beyond, beyond any adjective except possibly existence, a mystery as dark as the energy locked up in a lump of coal. And beyond that are mysteries and realities pointed to by cabbala (Jewish mystical tradition) but beyond our understanding or even our imagination.

In this vast perspective, I began to see a place for all my God-bits and experiences and how they interlocked into a reality beyond them all. It came to my mind through the writings of Swami Vivekananda, the first Hindu missionary to the West, who went to a conference in Chicago at the end of the nineteenth century and never returned to his homeland.

He sets out the different ways to reach the Divine in a few pamphlets with unassuming titles. One is intellectual and is concerned with the path of intellect and truth.

Another way is through our feelings, and is about how to love not just those who love us but everybody and everything. Another is the humble, human but surest way to holiness, through integrity, duty and taking responsibility for the world. Yet another way is through the conquest of the body – hatha and rajah yoga. Later on, I realised there are other ways too, through sex and kundalini yoga, but these I was too Western to comprehend. At last I had found a religious way plotted by experience, not dogma.

I immediately recognised Christianity in this scheme – it was bhakti yoga, the way of love. The place of Judaism too was clear, with its myriad obligations and duties, whose observance makes you holy. It was the finest example of karma yoga, the path of responsibility and duty. Of course, every religion includes all the types listed by Vivekananda though it usually favours the route set out at its beginning by its founder. So though Judaism and Christianity have their particular ways, jnana (spiritual knowledge) devotees like Maimonides and Thomas Aquinas and other egghead characters find an intellectual way specially for them. In any case, people change their approach in the course of their life according to their spiritual needs.

My Judaism and Christianity were now two means to the same end which I could use to fertilise each other or destroy each other. I am grateful that with me they have done the former. Even Marxism had its place. In Jewish tradition, God says, 'If only they would forget me but keep my commandments.' One rabbi said that atheism too had its purpose. 'When a poor man comes before you, do not say "God will look after you" but act as if there were no God, and you were the only one in the world who could help him.'

This classification of Vivekananda helped me also to understand myself and my first congregations. Some wanted lots of liturgy, loaded with pious objects. Like all lovers, they needed romance as I had done myself. Biblical criticism was irrelevant to them. Some needed committees where they could learn to work, not for their egos but for something higher. Services in the sense of prayers could never be central for them. Some needed to refine their prejudices and learn to listen for the sake of truth, and 'God is truth' as the Jewish liturgy says.

Understanding these different yoga ways, I ceased to be fanatical about style. 'God,' as the Moslems repeat again and again, 'is greater!'

My swami in North London also recommended the *Bhagavad-Gita*, and I read it in Christopher Isherwood's translation which charmed me with its Hiawatha rhythm. In the story, the problems of the hero turn inside out (as they had done with me) under the guidance of his charioteer, who turns out too as the incarnation of the God Krishna. You can read about all that yourself. What was important for me was how the Divine incarnates itself constantly. This fitted my own experience. I had witnessed the Divine doing just that in Grandma, the moon, my dog, Jesus in Galilee, the heroes and heroines of the Holocaust, in Josephine Butler in Liverpool, in Bede. They were all types of Emmaus experience.

Of course, people change their religion, and for many years I earned my living in the Jewish establishment by helping unbelieving Christians become contented Jews and by being understanding to Jews who were going in the other direction to groups and sects, some of which I'd visited myself.

When you like something, you want to apologise for everything in it. But I found to my pleasure that I had outgrown such childlike oversimplification. I am deeply grateful for what Hinduism had to offer but I don't have to take on board its caste system, its many self-appointed, self-hypnotised human divinities (the few genuine ones were quietly stunning), and its cavalier attitude to Western scientific and technical knowledge, which it never rightly appreciated but only thought it did. Still, thank you and thank you again!

I was told two morsels of Vedanta which remain in my mind and which I meditate on still: the dancing girl at the maharajah's court who whispered to Vivekananda, 'Do not despise me, for I am also holy.' And also this conundrum set by a sage. 'This mind is like the screen of a cinema and images and shadows flit across it. Who is the projector?' I had hardly begun to unpack such depths and heights in me!

Christians consider Jesus as the only incarnation, which I understand because it is the mark of every lover for whom the beloved will always be the only one for him or her.

Later on, I read a children's book of great spiritual wisdom, *The Little Prince*, by Antoine de Saint-Exupéry. It tells the story of the love between the little prince and his rose. The rose cannot believe that the little prince will still love her if he finds out that she is no longer unique, but that there are other roses, whole planets of them. But he does. In the same way, religions cannot believe in the completeness of their own revelation if God is in other revelations too. But they should, because he is and the evidence is before their eyes!

After this contact with Hindu Vedanta, theological purity no longer concerned me much. (It had never really worried me. It was what people said ought to worry me.) Thinking about it on a retreat, it seemed that Judaism was my home, Christianity was my 'affur, affur, *affaire*' and Vedanta was the frame into which everything fitted.

All knowledge is partial – religious as well as scientific. We do not know how the different parts of knowledge fit together – how we turn scientific knowledge into personal integrity and goodness. The scientific discipline requires a special type of integrity, but this did not prevent Hitler's scientists using their science for bogus scientific, racial purposes or their own discoveries for mass murder.

Religion which might be, ought to be, helpful has its own problems in this regard – how to recognise myth and mythical history in its own stories. At present, it only recognises such things in the myths of other faiths. As one weary and cynical professor told me at the beginning of my studies, Jews are believers when they study the Old Testament and biblical critics when they study the New, and with Christians, of course, it is the same but the other way round. And continuing this thought, Moslems are critics of both but their own, of course, is infallible in a different way from those which come after.

If you stay in your own religion from childhood it is not necessary to think such thoughts. But I had wandered, as had many, many others, and I could not unknow what I did know and become the classic repentant sinner. I had not sinned – far from it! My voyages were a virtue. I was forced to think fresh thoughts about situations my forefathers had not experienced. I had to go on ahead.

Judaism and Christianity find such ecumenical leaps difficult. They tried and the 'Noachide laws' and 'invincible ignorance' are crude but well-meant attempts to recognise the obvious, the open secret, that there are revelations and brands of goodness other than their own.

The problem is that Judaism and Christianity are too

146

closely related. Both use the logic that the more right I am, the less right you can be. This faulty logic works within them too and traditionalist groups use it against progressive ones – and, of course, vice versa.

Eastern logic was my liberation. I do not know how I stumbled over Swami Vivekananda's books but when I read them I did not learn a new truth, I recognised it. The pieces were already in place in my mind. The truth could even overcome the occasional mawkishness and antimacassar Victorianism in those books. Vivekananda was also more at home with Christianity than he was with Judaism (or Islam). But I no longer had to pretend perfection in any way or any person, whether Marx, Moses, Jesus, Reich or Vivekananda, whether in the Old Testament, New Testament, *The Function of the Orgasm* or *Das Kapital*. About the same time incidentally, I 'forgave' my parents in analysis for not being perfect parents. They shouldn't have tried so hard.

One day at a Vedantist meeting, to my surprise I bumped into a fellow rabbinical student who told me about his own guru and we compared notes. He also told me of another rabbi on the same track. It was all rather hush-hush but it was nice having company.

I was intrigued by Vivekananda's words about Buddhism, which I had never explored before. I filed it away in my mind for a future spiritual journey, because it said things I already recognised. It made me curious about Buddhism. The Divine would doubtless show its hand.

22

A Meditation on the Concourse of Euston Station

The Baal Shem Tov refused to go into a certain synagogue because so many insincere prayers had been said there, it stifled him.

Chassidic story

Though it is not our duty to finish the task, we are not permitted to give it up.

The Talmud – The Sayings of the Fathers

I don't get as much out of formal services now as I used to – at least, not in the way I was meant to. There's nothing unnatural in that. I've just taken too many, edited too many and composed too many and I feel like a human prayer wheel. For the moment, I'm prayed through and prayed out. God may feel equally flat, over-saturated with all the compliments I've pickled him in. On the other hand, some services feel more and more right to me. They are the intimate, informal table services of Jewish tradition, where I revert to childhood. Of course, I no longer try and see angels entering our kitchen, bringing us each a Sabbath present of a new soul (the old ones have got grubby during the week). Yet I do feel their presence around the table, because I can feel the holiness from another dimension forming us into a family. It requires no belief. You can sense it in our voices and behaviour.

I don't need religious romance as I used to, either. My love life is satisfying in quantity and quality, and sublimation is no longer necessary. The divine hasn't disappeared but is interwoven in the fabric of my unremarkable daily life.

That is why I meditate, contemplate, think, feel and pray where that daily life is richest – not in synagogues, churches or chapels but in places where there is less expectation, such as departure lounges, hospital waiting-rooms, on London double-decker buses and sitting in the concourses of big London stations. There, I'm moved by the arrivals and departures, the businessmen, the beggars, ladies anxious about their luggage and students looking like Rumpelstiltskin under their backpacks. As seen through the eyes of God, they seem so holy!

I often go to such places because though these services no longer work as prayer, they are my own introduction and a diving board into it. Sitting in Euston Station, one of the words I recited so easily in the synagogue service starts to reverberate in me like a bell and I listen as I once listened to the bells in Oxford, trying to hear what it is calling me to. The communal statements of the formal service begin to yield their personal message to me.

I'm not alone. Lots of people feel like me. They also need not just religion but spirituality, a direct line to God, the Divine, their own soul. Spirituality is a word that's not been used much in Judaism. I don't think my Yiddish grandparents would have even heard about it – only commandments and their fulfilment. But for more and more modern believers it's not a luxury but functional for living.

For many of them, concentration on the fulfilment of commandments by itself doesn't necessarily lead to kindness, generosity, love for those who disagree with you and tolerance. Mathematical religion (the one who fulfils the greatest number of commandments gets the prize) can lead to the opposite, to self-righteousness and one-upmanship. The mechanical religious result is not attractive, so people turn to inner spirituality, not just religion.

For some people, formal religion no longer fits their life situation. It didn't mine. But though ecclesiastics didn't come to my aid, God did and he lifted me and my problem into another dimension.

For many, the old authority has changed. Bibles can no longer be read without biblical criticism and their texts cannot be interpreted with medieval, rabbinic logic, great though that was in its day. New authority also needs an inner scripture, a spiritual experience of life.

After the Holocaust, many people no longer believe in God who is Lord of Hosts, and commander of history. Perhaps he was there but asleep or snoozing. Such a God is not worth praying to, which is why they are outside religion. Yet some cannot leave it like that. Perhaps they have been looking for God in the wrong place. They wonder if they ought to have looked inside themselves.

Many good people still stay comfortably in their childhood faith quite naturally, though I couldn't nor could people like me. They will find this book curious but irrelevant. Many who have lost their faith in traditional religion will wonder why I still bother flaying a dead horse. The relics of present-day religions, the formal services in under-used places of secularised worship, dot the landscape like memorials to dying cults.

I myself have found a religious home in non-orthodox

Judaism. Therefore this book will give most to believers in search of a spiritual home which is not a prison. It may even help old-time believers who suppress their secret similarity to the likes of me. There are many of these because modern fundamentalism includes an undeclared suppression of an inner truth, whether psychological or critical. Their aggression is the giveaway.

These are the characteristics of free-range believers. We are not religious battery birds. We live in an open society and have not fenced off our childhood faith from truth, or surrounded it with a quarantine zone. We have attended exotic services, chanted unfamiliar prayers on other people's retreats, dropped into lectures which would have shocked our grandparents. We are the modern travellers, pilgrims and students, seeking teachers like the wandering scholars of the Middle Ages. We try to adapt the divine wisdom of a closed society to the needs of an open one. Doubt is our opportunity, not our enemy.

But when we have found a pearl of great price, we bring it back to our religious home to join the tradition which we inherited, to enrich it with new life and fresh experience. That is our faithfulness. This has always happened in Judaism, though now it is conscious when once it was not. The battery birds may call us assimilationists, traitors, eclectics, Gentile lovers, or goyish (the same sneer but in Yiddish). But our own individual highest factor is more trustworthy than any communal lowest common denominator (in practice, this means religious nationalism).

After my inner Christian experience, I didn't become Christian. I returned to my native Judaism instead, but my Judaism is not the same since that experience.

What propels us forward is need. The test of what we

find is, Does it work? Does it make us more generous and deeper in our understanding? Does it help us locate God in ourselves? Does the divine spark light up in us? Christianity did that for me in the fifties. It gave me an inner voice, divine love, paradox and heaven. I have expressed my gratitude by bringing these gifts back to my Jewish home, dispensing with the labels. How these 'gifts' will be understood or integrated I cannot tell.

My thirty-five years' experience as a rabbi tells me there is a need for an adaptation of all of these gifts, because most Jews now make their own selection from their rabbinic past – some select more, some select less. Jews now need to find answers to problems their ancestors never faced. And those answers cannot be found in books or in archaeology or in politics, but in themselves, if they risk it. The alternative is communalism, ancestor-worship or respectability.

The Holocaust and the last war, which murdered so much good, also indiscriminately shattered some bad things too. Politically, I doubt if there will ever be a Franco-German war again, which brought tragedy to Europe and the world three times in one lifetime. Religiously, both the hot war between Christians and Jews and the cold war which succeeded it are dying too – please God, for good! Perhaps it is because the religious Middle Ages are dying as well. The bill for pious, religious prejudice and bad scholarship was too shocking. Uncritical, unselfcritical religion can no longer be our self-indulgence. Its present horrific consequences shriek out at us, not just in Israel and Palestine, but in Northern Ireland, Afghanistan and Bosnia too.

But what does 'belonging' mean, since the hippy days? My grandparents 'belonged' because they all tried to keep the same practices at the same time and didn't stray. But 'belonging' for me and my generation means being connected to our religion by a long cord of elastic with a lot of stretch. Religion is a search, a pilgrimage, not a fortress. We want to build bridges, not fences or ghettos, even self-imposed ones.

Browse through the newspapers in the kiosk at the station, listen to the news on your radio. In Hebron and Jerusalem, modern versions of old-time believers are still erecting old-time fences, and the hatred is becoming endemic. It is the same all over the globe. Scientific wisdom has progressed while the religious kind has remained primitive, using state force where it cannot persuade. God hasn't grown up with his devotees. So religion now is both a cure and the very illness it seeks to cure.

There is a lot of religious growing up to do. God is not our fall guy. Many years ago someone showed me a cartoon which expressed this succinctly. I think it was by Steinberg, and it showed a man in midair, holding himself up by his own extended hand which stretched under his feet. 'Who am I,' said the man, 'to have an opinion of my own?' That cartoon made a great impression on me.

But another scripture has revealed itself to us in our own time, different in style from previous ones which are paraded and processed in services. It has not come from above but has seeped upwards from our inner voice, and our self-understanding, often through the discipline of analysis, therapy or counselling. It is our private scripture, which needs to be set alongside the public Scriptures of official faith.

After all the tides of feeling that I have described, this is what remains for me. I come back to it again. There is a power of redemption at work in me, in you and in the world outside, which makes the crooked straight. For many reasons I began to experience that power as personal, dwelling in me and in others, alive and dead, some historical, some mythical, some imaginary and some all three. It redeemed me from bitterness and anger.

For me, life itself has been the great scripture. It has to validate other scriptures, their apologetics and theology. Fortunately, I have dealt with too many inbuilt problems to play games or indulge in religious one-upmanship. I am too poor in spirit to spurn any bit of redemptive experience just because it happens to wear the wrong label or comes at me from an unexpected direction. Marx, Kropotkin, Jesus, Freud, Reich and Reform Judaism have been my angel guides, who have between them made me into an inconsistent but more creative and affectionate human being and redeemed me from being institutionalised. It would be discourteous and imprudent to deny any of them.

Jesus didn't solve all my problems. He couldn't even solve his own. But at a 'crucial' moment in my life, he turned my bitterness into blessing and through him I plugged into a circuit of love. My analyst at the same time welded that into the reality of the outer world and common sense, rescuing me from the solipsism which fantasists like me inhabit. All my guides continue to work in me, saving me from hardness of heart and neurosis. What comes next I don't know. Jesus must have some pondering to do as well as me. He's also had a lot of growing up to do since the Gospels.

Suddenly, I open my eyes and look around the concourse, and it is *as if* my friend is sitting opposite me, making me laugh as he parodies my uptight self-righteousness, my pomposity and my theorising. The kingdom of heaven doesn't come like that.

My Affair with Christianity

I try to separate myself from such sanctimoniousness by gazing at the real world. I give my inner eye a rest and notice with my real eyes that boutiques have replaced benches in modern stations. The great, glitzy and good have their lounges, the rest of us can consume and stand. I get up and leave my coveted seat empty for whoever's lucky enough to grab it and buy three sandwiches. One is for me, another for a beggar and another for a French student who is obviously down to her last penny, like I used to be. It's sentimental stuff but a bit of heaven begins to open up, which is the test. The old magic/mythology still works. Inner voices make some people pretty weird. But to me they brought good. Thanks!

23

Whoever, Whatever, Esq.

What is man that thou art mindful of him?
Psalm 8:4

Teilhard de Chardin thought we human beings were the
first animals on the evolutionary scale who were able to
get beyond their senses and regard spiritual realities as
really real. That isn't easy for us and explains why we are
such a mixed-up lot.

Our fridges and freezers are real – there is no doubt
about that – and so are the hamburgers and portions of
duck à l'orange that fill them. And so are our second cars
if we've made it, and our dole handouts if we haven't.
But what about infinity, eternity, heaven, souls, angels,
conscience and God? Can they ever be really real?

Yet, when our second cars crash, and the value of our
windfall shares goes with the wind, and we have to come
to terms with the break-up of our bodies, it is the strength
of those non-sensible realities which we call upon to save
us from breakdown, depression and the bottle.

But there is a problem. We have no precise language to
describe them or our own experience of them. Our
ordinary language, which serves us so well in business
and with cars, fridges and windfall shares is inadequate.
This has been a problem in writing this book. This is why

my language has wandered from popular romances to scraps of psychological theory and theological abstractions. None of them works properly.

I say I am in love with whoever, whatever. We converse and feel close. It is as if I am sitting on one side of a sofa *as it were*, and whoever, whatever, esq. is snuggling up just beside me *as it were*. But this cannot be. Whoever, whatever is more than close. She/him/it is God in me or his image, and I am in her/him/it. It is not ordinary romance after all, because my lover is see-through and so is my soul. We are a paradoxical pair of lovers.

We cannot help it, because all we say about God, eternity and infinity can only be paradoxical and half-truths, and even that is being generous. There are two possibilities. We can either make use of the language of abstraction, which seems too distant and cold to express what we feel, or use the language of the imagination, which can seem so mawkish that you may want to retch as you read it.

I have used the latter because my experience of non-sensed reality took the form of a love affair, though the object of my love was mainly within me and part of me. It was and it wasn't a kind of self-love. That is the problem and the paradox.

It was the experience which was important. The language and labels I leave to you.

It is said that a computer was constructed in Jerusalem which could translate the Scriptures from any language into any language. Eagerly the scholars tested it and fed into it the text, 'The spirit is willing but the flesh is weak.' The computer considered this and came up with, 'The gin is full strength but the beef is flabby.'

That's the distance between my words and my experience. Be indulgent, if this book is to benefit you!

24

The Greatest Gift

As I travel through the bad and good,
Keep me travelling the way I should.
Where I see no way to go,
You'll be travelling with me, I know.
    And it's from the old I travel to the new
    Keep me travelling along with you.
Sidney Carter

Be with me in my heart
    and in my loving.
Be with me at my end
    and at my departing.

It's taken me a lifetime to find out what I'm really like. One instance! I had always had a horror of being walked out on. And yet when I think back to the deepest relationships in my life, I have to admit that I myself have done my share of the walking out, which does nothing for my self-esteem. But my therapist and inner voice have between them made an honest rabbi of me. So I'm pleased I can admit this to myself and to you, which makes me feel better.

In my spiritual relationship I was equally disconcerted. I had harboured a nagging thought that some day I might have to dump my friend – not dump him exactly, just let his voice die down in me because it was intellectually embarrassing, or too demanding, or it didn't fit ecclesiastically. But it didn't happen that way – the reverse, in fact. He dumped me!

It happened, curiously enough, on a retreat where I had gone to deepen our relationship and enjoy a mystical love-in. The morning service had ended, and the candles had been extinguished, which suited me fine because the inner conversation gets better when there's less furniture around. And now came the glorious, companionable silence I was waiting for, like the enticing, glittering water of a swimming-pool before you, the first, dive in and break the surface. In such emptiness, voices may be heard and visions happen.

But what happened was an anti-happening. Just as I was wondering where to dive in, all the colour, all the spirituality, drained out of that chapel, out of the other meditators and out of me. The chapel reverted to a room, and my fellow-meditators to mumbling, muttering men and women. The eternal light was just a light – low wattage. There was nothing there. It was emptier than I had ever known it. And I was empty too. I tried once, twice, three times to get the spiritual juices flowing, but I was just bored. In the end, I gave up, I retreated, really retreated, packed my bags and took the train back to London.

On the train, I felt jilted and I panicked. I tried to puzzle out whey my inner voice had walked out on me. Could I cope without my old mate who had accompanied me to saunas, synagogues and bars? Had I annoyed him? Had I upset him? Though after all we had been through together this didn't seem likely. He wasn't the type.

I reverted to childhood insecurity. Perhaps if I said

some prayers three times, he'd listen. Perhaps I'd got to try harder. I screwed up my eyes and concentrated on the cabbalah, Etty Hillesum, and all my other mystical high-fliers. But it was no use. I'd have to accept the loneliness. My old mate had fallen into a black hole. Life in future would be very lonely and much less exciting. I would no longer see infinity in people's faces.

But like my mother I was a survivor, and Judaism came to my aid, because in Judaism feelings are luxuries and voices unnecessary. It is the good deeds which register. I remembered with relief that night that when I had got to London my charity hadn't disappeared with him. Instead of giving coins though, I gave away chocolate bars and sandwiches, which I had had to queue up for and were more trouble. But I no longer did it to please God, my friend, my voice, my guardian angel – just out of human pity and compassion and the thought that there but for the chances of life go I.

I also noticed that because there was nobody around inside me, I felt much freer. I no longer had to pray. I no longer had to drop into chapels or recite memorial prayers when an undertaker's car passed by. I no longer had to recite the same prayers before going to bed. If I had to be my own hotline to heaven, I'd just have to work harder at it, that's all.

But I still asked myself, Why, why, why? When we were getting on so nicely, too!

An answer came years later, during the rearrangement of my office. For many years, my secretary and I shared a tiny office as we administrated our department of canon law. We had known each other since childhood and there was a lot of love and laughter in our gossip. She had supported me through tempestuous times and she said I had taught her a thing or two about life as well. But my organisation grandly bought an ex-convent. It was our poor man's Vatican, and my department was allocated two rooms, not one – a large room for my secretary and me, which would do us both nicely, and a smaller anteroom where our clients could sit.

'It's going to be so nice,' I said to her, 'sharing such a big room.'

I felt rejected and disconcerted once again when she said, 'Lionel, this time we're going to have separate rooms. It's much better for the interviews. I need some private space too, and now you've got Jim you can cope without me.'

I felt the same panic as I had felt in the chapel. Once again, I was on my own. But I knew she was right, though I didn't like admitting it. I had reached the further slope of middle age and it was high time for me to grow up. I could get by in life without props now or having to hold someone's hand, whether solid or see-through.

The two rejections linked up in my mind. Now I knew why my voice had walked out on me. I could have cried with relief. It wasn't fed up with me. It wasn't annoyed, upset or angry. Kindness, pity and compassion no longer needed imagination or a myth, that's all. They came to me naturally without a mediator or an experience. I could go it alone. If I invoked my friend under a personal guise it wasn't necessarily because I needed him but because I thought he might need me. I was even sufficiently self-reliant to 'come out' to my friends.

I was even able now to 'come out' to them in another way, describing what had happened to me spiritually. I felt very foolish telling other people I'd been walked out on by a phantom. One of them told me helpfully that this happened to all upper-grade mystics. She cited dark nights of the soul, and the cloud of unknowing. A Jungian therapist was blunter and more basic. I was growing up, that's all – maturating, which made me feel like a cucumber in pickle.

I began to understand why such walk-outs have to happen. Without them you will grow but your religion won't, which will result in breakdown, abandoning religion altogether or retreating into fundamentalism to paper over the cracks. Some think they will become innocent if they refuse to grow, but they just become naive and artificial instead. Religion then descends into politics and power games. Someone told me that the Chinese ideogram for problem also means opportunity. I know no Chinese but it sounds right.

So now I'm waiting for whatever, whoever to show its hand. I know the Divine is quite close but in a direction I'm not used to looking. But it's always around, so I can wait. Occasionally, I imagine I glimpse him from afar as it were, but I know I've got to get along without him – to 'maturate', as the lady said. Perhaps he is the beggars I gave those chocolates and sandwiches to. Perhaps so much of him is inside me and part of me that I don't need him outside me – I assume him. Perhaps I now see him within other people and as part of them.

What form he will take I do not know. Perhaps both of us have gone further than forms. Perhaps he is only light. Perhaps he is burrowing away deep inside me to bring some love and light to my rejected and hidden self. Perhaps he is and always was me, so we can never be separated. But he follows me like the moon, my child-hood companion, so I don't feel lonely.

In any case, there will be that meeting when I get to this world's end. I'm prepared to bet on it, not just with my money but with me.

And I'm grateful, because my friend has left me the

most unselfish gift of all, my freedom. I wish I knew how to use it.

God bless!